Mega Mind

Path to Success and Freedom

Dear Tim
   The ability to create anything is within us all. It is upto us to access it.

   Thanks for your support

   Dr. Hemant Thakur.

Realize phenomenal success with a tool you already possess but may need to upgrade

MEGA MIND

Path to Success and Freedom

Your key to Happiness, Health, Wealth, Love and Innovation

Hemant Thakur, M.D.

"Problems of mankind are created by man. Solutions to those problems are within us."

Rutledge Books, Inc. Danbury, CT

Copyright © 2000 by Hemant Thakur, M.D.

ALL RIGHTS RESERVED
Rutledge Books, Inc.
107 Mill Plain Road, Danbury, CT 06811
1-800-278-8533
www.rutledgebooks.com

Manufactured in the United States of America

Thakur, Hemant
    Mega Mind: Path to Success and Freedom
    ISBN: 1-58244-075-1

    1. Motivation 2. Setting Goals 3. Self Help 4. Happiness

Library of Congress Card Number: 00-100933

Warning!

This book will change your life. Before modifying your diet, exercise program or medications please consult your personal physician. A board-certified physician or psychiatrist should also be consulted regarding cessation of serious drug or alcohol abuse.

"Hemant's advice on goal setting caused me to reassess the direction for my life. In looking hard at my priorities, I realized it was time for a major overhaul, particularly in the area of my life's work. I completed my projects, returned to college, and am now training for a new exciting career in one of the helping professions. It's never too late to make a life change, and none of us are too old to improve ourselves. Thanks Hemant!"

— L.M. Callaly, Carbondale, IL

"As Vietnam War veterans we wish to express our deepest respect and appreciation for Dr. Hemant Thakur. He has developed new techniques, which has changed the lives of many for the better. His seminars are educational and yet very entertaining. His approaches are easier to understand. These techniques can be used by anyone to improve their life in holistic ways." — Vietnam War Veterans

"I enjoyed reading Dr. Thakur's book. It was entertaining, but most importantly it made a lot of sense. I wish all kids my age could read it."

— Alanna Stanhope, Victoria, Australia

" It has been an honor to listen to Dr. Thakur's lecture and presentation based on his book Mega Mind. He has fascinating information, and practical techniques to improve the life in many areas. He is also an interesting and entertaining speaker, who gets his audience involved in his presentation." — Dr. Vladimir Golubovsky, M.D.
Chief of the Psychiatry Division Municipal Integrated Clinic
Yekaterinburg, Russia

"Your book helps all people how to find a right way in their actions to succeed in modern life. Your book should be useful to many people who are trying to improve their health, energy level, financial status or relationships. I am absolutely sure that your book and knowledge are applicable to the different people living in different countries as well as your experiences. — Nickolay N. Melnick, Esq.
Attorney at law with Inter-Republican Barrister's Association
Yekaterinburg Russia

About the Author

Hemant Thakur, M.D.

Dr. Hemant Thakur is a medical doctor; an assistant clinical professor and psychiatrist with specialized training in psychosomatic medicine, and a specialist in post-traumatic stress disorder (PTSD). He has worked as a psychiatrist in various mental health settings including Riker's Island Prison in New York City and many alcohol and drug rehabilitation programs. Dr. Thakur is also a United States Army officer, businessman, and inventor. His family includes a teen-aged son and daughter.

Born in Bombay, India, Dr Thakur emigrated to the United States in 1981. Apart from the barriers of language and culture, he also encountered numerous personal problems. Finally, after much adversity, he arrived at a point in his life where he decided to study what it is that makes people successful. He also studied many prominent people who have overcome enormous obstacles.

After years of treating people whose lives were in ruins, he saw that traditional psychiatry, drug therapies and psychotherapies were not always effective and when they did work, the results were not long lasting. He learned that unless these people were taught to give a different perception to their problems, they would not be free of the disempowering effects of past trauma, painful life experiences and problems, nor would they be able to handle new stresses and challenges in life. Thus, they could not be truly happy or successful human beings. He began to identify simple methods that changed behavior, solved life problems and minimized stress. He used these methods on himself and found that they are within reach of everyone. By making better choices these methods can help to start new, productive and, most importantly, happy lives. As a result, he now teaches these techniques in seminars and lectures. He also is the inventor of a patented product which is currently sold in the USA and Australia. You may visit his invention by visiting his Web site: http://www.galaxymall.com/health/breathace. He also has numerous ideas for future inventions.

Trauma, stress, and learned behavior influence every life to one degree or another and Dr. Thakur had to heal himself to be successful and happy. The premise of this book, then, is: If these techniques can help those traumatized from the worst possible experiences, they can help ordinary people conquer stress, overcome fear, break bad habits, achieve success, and reach a maximum level of self-actualization and happiness. This book will show you how to empower yourself with the hidden tools that you possess within yourself. This book will show you how!

Table of Contents

i. Acknowledgements xi

1. Mega-Mind: Introduction 1
2. Hit the Bull's-Eye Every Time 13
3. Actions for Success 35
4. The Two Masters: Driving Human Behavior 53
5. Action vs Inaction 81
6. Conditioned Responses 87
7. Empowering Meaning to Any Event 107
8. State of Mind 123
9. Emotional Record 133
10. Play a New Song 139
11. Focus Your Attention 145
12. Weight Reduction 151
13. Anger Management 159
14. Governing Values 165
15. Belief : Empowering or Disempowering? 173
16. Opportunities to Grow 185
17. Improving Energy and Health 195
18. Meditation 209
19. Power within You 215

Bibliography 229
The Story Behind Veterans for Humanity, Inc. 233

ACKNOWLEDGMENTS

I would like to express my deep appreciation to Lynn Callaly, who encouraged me to write this book based upon my seminars. I sincerely thank her, as well as Janet Corber, for reviewing this book and helping me put the enormous amount of information in book form.

For my children, Pooja and Neil, who have always inspired me and were so supportive in helping me work on this book, my love and thanks.

To Bernadette Stanhope, my friend from Australia who feels this book will make changes in millions of people's lives, my thanks for her encouragement and support. My appreciation and thanks to Ms. Stanhope and to Myrna Santiago for helping me realize the unique spiritual aspects of my work and myself.

Appreciation goes to Nancy Forth Logan and DeAnna Roberts for their help and support on this project.

I want to thank the thousands of veterans of the Second World War, Korean War, Vietnam War, and Gulf War with whom I have had the honor to work. I have been deeply touched by the decades of pain and suffering they have undergone. It has been a challenge to teach these veterans the techniques from my book as their numerous problems inspired me to look for ways to help them. I sincerely appreciate their support and presence in my life, as I also appreciate thousands of other patients from all walks of life who posed a challenge to me to show them how to improve their lives.

HEMANT THAKUR, MD

I want to thank Lawrence Berkeley National Laboratory, Berkeley, California for granting permission to use their images and thanks to Allyn and Bacon of Boston, Massachusetts for permission to use information on phychoneuroimmunology. Also, thanks to the Food and Nutrition Information Center of Beltsville, Maryland for letting me use information on nutrition.

Lastly, I want to thank my publisher, Rutledge Books, Inc., and editor, Barbara Fandrich, whose hard work has made this project successful.

Chapter 1

Mega-Mind: Introduction

The space exploration vehicle Voyager left the Earth, taking records of humanity for any intelligent life it might encounter on its intergalactic sojourn. NASA included a golden record of life on Earth with greetings in the many spoken languages of Earth, and simple line drawings of man, woman, and child. Future space probes may be armed with sound and video clips telling the whole history of life here, along with the great deeds of mankind. Who will be the representatives of Earth's greatness?

The space probe's journey is symbolic of our own path through life. All of us start simply with the same basic physical equipment, but very few realize a level of import so great that our philosophy or actions would be recorded as a pinnacle of human accomplishment. Why is this? Why are only a few precious individuals able to achieve fabulous breakthrough results, while others just pass through, fulfilling no particular destiny? Too many are unable to complete even the basic tasks of life due to physical or mental illness, a breakdown of their wills, or because they surrender to obstacles in their paths.

We all possess the same equipment, modified to a greater or lesser degree by heredity, disease, trauma, and experience. The most gifted genius ever tested and recorded did not vary that many points from millions of people possessed of average intelligence, and a high IQ does not guarantee great success or happiness. Great deeds often are produced by men and women of average intelligence, and there is no evidence that scoring below average intelligence will influence one's life negatively. At this stage in scientific development, by taking good care of our bodies many of us can live to age one hundred, but the average maximum age hovers around seventy-two. No matter what we do, we cannot at the present time hope for a fantastic span of years, like five or six hundred years. It is fair to say that we all have the same physical equipment, similar brains driving the parts, and about the same warranty.

Let us examine just what we all possess in the way of equipment. Even when we sit down to relax, the body performs six trillion reactions per second! Our hearts beat one hundred thousand times a day, our lungs breathe oxygen in and out more than twenty-five thousand times per day, and our bodies exchange oxygen in billions of cells every second. Two hundred billion red cells are normally destroyed and replaced each day. The adult human body contains something on the order of one hundred trillion cells, which are organized and differentiated to form a number of different kinds of tissue with specific functions. Our cells send out signals to all parts of the body and blood rushes through thousands of miles of vessels and arteries. **How is it that our bodies are able to coordinate trillions of reactions in a second? Were we to try to consciously organize six trillion reactions, we would not survive even a few seconds.**

The achievers of Earth selected to represent all humanity on future space probes, such as Martin Luther King, Jr. and Mahatma Gandhi, were no different at a physical level than you or me. Most lacked genius-level IQs and were not possessed of great physical prowess. What made them achieve phenomenal results in their lives? They had the same physical equipment, perhaps average or slightly above-average brains, and sometimes less than a maximum lifespan. You can no doubt think of a hundred special achievers in every walk of life: Bill Gates, Henry Ford, Hapsburg Empress Maria Theresa, Thomas Edison, Madame Curie, John Glenn, General Colin Powell, Ted Turner, Anthony

INTRODUCTION

Robbins—the list is long and distinguished. What special intelligence, knowledge, or energy do these people tap into to produce amazing and sometimes world-changing results?

This book shows you step-by-step how to recognize the special essence of success, learn it, and master it.

 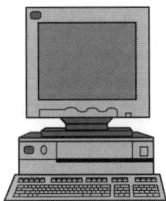

These computers look identical and indeed all the physical components are the same. Why does the computer on the left take five minutes to process an image, while the one to the right takes only seconds? The first computer's processor is the old 386DX technology, while the second has been upgraded to the new MMX Technology. In an hour, the computer on the left can be upgraded to the newer faster processor. If it were possible to boost your ability to think, act, learn, and achieve as easily as upgrading your personal computer, would you do so? **If you could change the software in your brain in order to create phenomenal results, would you get the new software?**

Two friends speed down the highway in cars which look identical in every way-same make, model, year, and condition. Why does one friend pass the other as if he were standing still? When the slower driver reaches his destination, he asks his friend how he achieved such acceleration in the same car. After the requisite amount of teasing the friend reveals that he has replaced the original four-cylinder standard engine with a six-cylinder Porsche engine, which took the mechanic two days to install. **If you were able to increase your speed in moving, thinking, acting, and finishing the various journeys of your life with only a few days' work, would you?**

By the time you finish reading this book you will have the skills to accelerate your performance in virtually every aspect of your life, and it will not cost you as much as upgrading your PC or getting a new engine for your car. The only investment you will make is a conscious and continuing effort to put what you learn into action and eventually make it a conditioned response, something as routine and automatic as driving your car.

Lesson 1. Do Not Reinvent the Wheel!

Most of us drive and travel regularly in some sort of car, truck, or van. We just get into the vehicle, turn the key, and go. We don't build the car in order to drive it. If we had to do so, we would first have to learn how to make rubber for the tires, steel for the body, and master all the technologies for the working parts. In effect, we would be reinventing the wheel. If we had to make a car, most of us would miss a whole generation and never travel one mile! Being clever and putting a value on our time, we buy a vehicle and travel with ease wherever we wish to go. For some reason when faced with a new challenge or setting a new goal, we are not so clever and often try to reinvent the wheel. We stumble around, start and stop, and not surprisingly years pass too quickly and we have nothing to show for our efforts. Let us use the method our brain already knows to travel from point A to point B. Every goal in life (losing weight, finding a job, getting married and making money, etc.) is a short trip, and we shouldn't have to reinvent the wheel to get there!

A cardiologist treated people whose arteries were clogged by high-fat fast food. Even after bypass surgery, many of his patients returned to their pattern of relying on fast food, knowing very well that it had contributed greatly to their cardiac problems. He realized that being terribly busy and over-burdened with responsibilities, the allure of fast food was all but irresistible. He had a marvelous idea to open a fast-food restaurant with

INTRODUCTION

tasty, low fat, and heart-healthy recipes. He and two other physicians got together and, pooling their resources, developed a business plan.

They studied drive-through buildings, ordering mechanisms, expensive four-color printing, and even hired an architect who had previously worked for McDonald's and Burger King franchises to design their first restaurant. They hired the best expensive lawyers to begin licensing the new company as a franchiser, and it looked like their new business idea would be a nationwide hit, make them very wealthy, and help the public at large eat healthier on the move. They paid a fast-food franchise-marketing expert to plan their grand opening, which garnered wide-reaching media coverage. Early reviews of the food indicated that it was not only healthy but also delicious. It looked like their success was assured. They enjoyed the excitement, but within the first year this consortium of physicians sought protection from their creditors. Why?

Being well-educated and distinguished professionals, they thought they were smarter than the competition. So, enthused by their early success, they failed to continue the weekly advertising and marketing plan developed by the expert. They chose other methods, like educating the public through articles on the benefits of healthy eating. These efforts were admirable and no doubt did impart important information to people who needed it, but it did not have the business effect of keeping customers driving through or dining in the restaurant every day. The daily costs of operation added up over several months, and the losses mounted. Even the good incomes of three talented physicians could not keep it going. Although they had paid top dollar to professionals with proven track records in the fast-food industry, they tried to reinvent the wheel when it came to marketing on an ongoing basis.

How many of us outsmart ourselves by doing the same in our own lives? We do it all the time, and a good education, high IQ, and even being well-heeled financially can't protect us from disaster if we try to reinvent the wheel. When it comes to ongoing marketing, this book provides several successful examples, how to understand them fully, and how to follow them exactly to succeed.

Finding the ideal life partner and keeping the relationship fresh and exciting, getting a good job, starting a business of our own, building a legacy for retirement and the next generation, creating maximum physical energy, living longer, coping with or eliminating physical or psychological pain, and feeling truly happy are challenges most of us would like to master. We cannot do so by reinventing the wheel. We can do it by recognizing our innate talents and abilities and taking stock of what we know that will support our life goals. Just as important, we need to know what we lack and set about gaining new knowledge and developing new behaviors that will make us succeed. We must identify and upgrade our technology, because it does exist. We must find the perfect recipe.

Lesson 2. Find a Recipe

I came from Bombay, India where I had never tasted pork or endured a harsh winter. An African-American friend invited me over for dinner on a blustery winter night and served ham and beans. The rich, hearty tastes took the edge off the chill and delighted my palate. My host explained that his recipe for ham and beans, created by his great-grandmother, was very simple and inexpensive to prepare. He gave me the ingredients, portions, and steps to make ham and beans anytime at my own home.

A few weeks later I decided to surprise another American friend with a meal of ham and beans at my house. I soaked the beans, followed all the steps conscientiously, but then decided to alter the portions and add other ingredients from India just to make it a little better. When my friend came over for dinner that night, I served dinner with great pride. Both of us eagerly dug into the ham and beans, only to recoil from the taste. It was awful! As I dialed to make reservations at a restaurant, I

INTRODUCTION

told my friend, "I'm really sorry I messed up the ham and beans, but I'm mystified about why this happened."

The next day I reported this disaster to my first friend who had provided the recipe. This friend asked if I had altered the recipe in any way, and I replied that I had purchased the best ingredients, measured everything correctly, followed the steps with care, but decided to add a little curry and turmeric while the pot simmered. The man said, "Hemant, you can't play with success! My great-grandmother perfected that recipe over a lifetime of cooking. Even though it's simple, you must follow it exactly as written to get a perfect pot of ham and beans."

We can apply this to a well-known business story. Colonel Sanders couldn't live comfortably on his retirement income so he decided to take his chicken recipe to world. He didn't have the capital to build or acquire more restaurants, so he began knocking on the doors of other restaurateurs with his formula. He knocked on more than a thousand doors before someone said, "Yes, I can do better with your formula."

We're talking about more than the recipe for Kentucky Fried Chicken here, it is a recipe for business success. If we have something special the public wants but we have limited capital, we must forge alliances to market our idea widely. If we want to succeed like Colonel Sanders, his recipe for success must be followed, no matter how challenging. If he'd quit after ten, one hundred, or even one thousand "nos" he would never have realized the one "yes" that made history. An important ingredient of the Colonel's success recipe was **persistence.**

I went through a similar challenging experience in my life, as a shy young doctor seeking a medical residency in the United States. I heard hundreds of "nos" from hospitals to which I had eagerly applied to be a resident, and had I been less dogged and determined I may have given up before asking the question the 401st time. The one "yes" I finally received from Mount Sinai of New York, after great pain to me personally enabled me to become a psychiatrist and change my life and the lives of others.

Often in life we are given a perfect recipe for success, but being intelligent and clever people we tamper with it in an attempt to make it better. **A perfect recipe includes ingredients, portions, and steps. If you want a perfect result, don't alter the recipe!**

Lesson 3. Set, Track and Realize Goals

New Year's Resolutions are made and broken without thought, or laughed off as silly ideas we are just not capable of carrying through. Throughout our lives many goals are set and discarded or genuinely pursued but not carried through to fruition. By setting goals casually and letting them slide we do ourselves a disservice. When we work diligently to achieve a goal only to lose in the end because of our own behavior, it can damage our self-esteem.

Losing weight and getting in shape is a perfect example. Only a few of us stay in peak physical condition. Sixty percent of Americans are overweight, and many try countless diets and weight-reduction schemes only to lose and regain weight again and again. Not only have they never realized their ideal weight and been able to maintain it, but they have lost years and a great deal of money fumbling around seeking solutions.

I know a woman (let's call her Linda), who has gained and lost the same fifty pounds ten times in twenty years! She tried the Dr. Atkins' diet, Nutri-systems, Jenny Craig, Weight Watchers, liquid diet/fasting, food combining, fenfluramine/phentermine (fen/phen), the rice diet, the grapefruit diet, and more - only to realize the same results. Not only is this frustrating and costly, but it can and often does do damage to the body. The yo-yo effect is common in people losing ten or more pounds, and is a source of exasperation, self-esteem issues, and complications to general

INTRODUCTION

health. Linda said, "But I wasn't trying to reinvent the wheel. I used recognized systems (recipes that have worked for others) and still failed. Why?"

Linda asked a legitimate question. She had identified, accessed, and practiced knowledge that had worked for millions of people. She realized success temporarily, which is often the case with addictive behaviors like overeating, smoking, alcohol or drug abuse, promiscuity, etc., only to relax after realizing her goal and regain the weight she had lost, with more pounds in most cases. It is important to understand why people overeat, abuse alcohol and drugs, engage in a promiscuous lifestyle, excessively shop or worry, and engage in many other obsessive/compulsive behaviors. Later we will explore the whys involved, but here we start with a simple goal to change behavior backed up by a daily record.

Goals must be set, a recipe identified and followed, and results checked and rechecked. For a lifelong problem like this, the goal must be kept in clear sight. A visual checklist makes this process real and forces us to monitor ourselves on a daily basis. Linda weighed 200 pounds and set a goal of reducing her weight to 150 pounds, and I instructed her to reinforce the process by keeping track of the activities she performed throughout the day that either support or thwart her goal. Asking a simple question as you begin any activity during the day will help keep you on track and moving toward your goal. At the end of the day, write it all down to make a visual record.

Ask yourself, **"Is this action supporting the realization of my goal?"** If you can honestly say "yes" then continue the activity. If you must say "no" then stop at once. It will take a while for you to turn this type of thinking into a conditioned response (an automatic habit), so at the end of the day you will have listed activities that both support and thwart your goals-until you have perfected the method. For example, it may be that your current habit is to return home from work, grab a bowl of potato chips and a couple of beers or Cokes, and sit down in front of the television for three or four hours before bed. Ask yourself each night, "Is this action supporting the realization of my goals?"

Of course it is not, so night after night until you break your harmful habits you must continue to ask the question. It is helpful to substitute better behaviors for the negative conditioned ones. Go ahead and watch television, but walk on a treadmill or ski machine or do exercises for at least one of the hours you spend in front of the screen. If you are hungry after your workout, get diet cola or bottled spring water and some low-fat popcorn. Day by day the destructive behaviors will be transformed into positive ones, until your conditioned response will be to automatically do the helpful activity.

Writing down your daily performance provides visual tracking of your progress. If you are diligent, day by day you will see the THWART column become shorter and the SUPPORT column grow longer. People reluctant to write such a record may object because of limitations of time, but this process takes less than five minutes near the end of every day. This is what one day's chart recorded in the middle of Linda's weight reduction program looked like:

Goal: To realize & maintain a weight of 150 lbs. for life
Progress: Weight = 170 lbs.
Date: Monday, January 26, 1999

Actions That SUPPORT My Goal

- Walked dog for 15 minutes before work.
- Exercised on Fitness Flyer for 15 minutes.
- Prepared salad with skinless chicken and low fat dressing.

Actions That THWART My Goal

- Ate french fries at lunchtime.
- Watched 4 hours of TV after work.
- Ate popcorn as late night snack, low-fat but ate the whole bag.

INTRODUCTION

Early in her weight-loss program, the activities that thwarted her goal far outweighed the actions that supported it. At the point of this daily record (almost halfway to her goal), the harmful and helpful activities were balanced. To continue on the right path, she must continue to add activities to the **SUPPORT** column and remove them from the **THWART** column. This principle can be applied to any goal in life, but must be repeated daily. Writing them down helps us to visually track our progress and to truly and permanently change our behavior.

Doctors, psychologists, lawyers, physicists, and engineers have as much trouble realizing their goals as housewives, clerical people, and computer operators. All have access to vast amounts of knowledge and recipes that will work if followed precisely, but knowledge is not enough. **Only action creates results**, and every action or inaction in the day impacts those results. A good recipe supported by a visual record of the daily actions that either support or thwart the goal can and will maximize the desired result.

We have learned in this chapter:

Lesson 1. **Do not reinvent the wheel.** We all are trying to get somewhere in life. Rather than start from zero and spend a lifetime building a mode of transportation that will work, we must find a set of wheels already in existence to propel us from point A to point B in any area of life.

Lesson 2. **Find a recipe**. Any and every problem you may be encountering in your life has been encountered and overcome by someone else. Find the person who has mastered a recipe to solve your particular challenge, study its ingredients, portions, and steps, and follow it exactly to achieve the same positive result.

Lesson 3. **Set, track and realize goals.** Anyone can set a goal or want something positive to happen, but it takes daily consistent actions, tracking, and a visual record to truly change our conditioned responses and negative behaviors and to make our goals real.

Most people live, whether physically, intellectually or morally, in a very restricted circle of their potential being. They make use of a very small portion of their consciousness, and of their possible consciousness, and of their soul's resources in general, much like a man who, out of his whole bodily organism, should get into a habit of using and moving only his little finger.

(William James)

Chapter 2

Hitting the Bull's-Eye Every Time

When learning archery, shooting, or golf, we don't just fire arrows, shells, and golf balls into space. We aim for a target at a specified distance. The archer aims her arrow to penetrate the smallest circle of a drawn target (traditionally the bull's-eye) yards away. The trapshooter yells "pull" and a clay bird or trap is released, at which he takes aim. He disintegrates the clay disk if a skilled marksman. The golfer tees off, hitting the ball with great force, but if the drive is not carefully aimed at the green he will land in the rough and not realize the target hole.

People who succeed keep their targets in mind all the time, never losing sight of the bull's-eye. Most of us amble through life, going with the flow, and fire off shots or drives whenever the spirit moves. This takes our energy, but without a target our aims just go into space never to realize any defined destination.

As discussed in Chapter 1, we all possess virtually the same equipment. We are composed of the same physical material whether Caucasian, Hispanic, Afro-Origin, Semitic, Native American, Indo-Pak, or Asian. All of our bodies require rest, and every day is twenty-four hours long. Most of us work and/or travel between eight and twelve of those hours per day. Many of us are overly "occupied" all the time without really getting anywhere. How often have you felt as if you were spinning your wheels? A small percentage of people realize extraordinary results working the same or even fewer hours; they don't spin their wheels or waste energy, they really go places.

We all have an abundance of potential, but precious few of us set precise written goals to get somewhere in life. The primary reason people fail to perform this pivotal action is that they don't know how. Surely if setting goals could make us happy, healthy, successful, and wise, why don't we all do so? It's like going on vacation. If you had no destination in mind you would spend the whole two weeks traveling around aimlessly. Your precious vacation time would be squandered and you would be depressed at having gone nowhere and done nothing useful with another full year of work in front of you. Just as you select a place to go on vacation, so must you set goals for your life. If you want to travel the path of life and reach ultimate success and fulfillment you should have a destination, a goal.

Twelve steps to achieving goals

Step 1 – *Write down your goals for all the important aspects of your life, even if some seem impossible.* You must not rely on vague thoughts in your head-you must make goals real and visual. It is wise to write goals for all areas of your life, because if you realize great success in one area and fail in some of the other areas, you will feel unsatisfied, out of balance, and unhappy-and that is not true success. If you make plenty of money but neglect your health, you will not be able to enjoy your wealth, travel, and enjoy your hard-won free time. If you climb to the top of the corporate ladder, but neglect your personal relationship with spouse or significant other, you may end up alone at the top of the heap. On the other hand, if you love your spouse passionately and put all your energy into your family at the expense of your career, you may end up without the resources to support your household, which leads to conflict and can destroy the early happiness. All areas must be worked together for a balanced, happy life.

The most comprehensive way to author your goals starts with questions and open-ended statements. You will no doubt be able to add many more questions and statements to this list, but if you answer all these questions and complete the statements you will be well on your

HITTING THE BULL'S-EYE EVERY TIME

Physical	Emotional	Financial	Relationship	Employment	Educational	Spiritual	Other
Weight	Get rid of anger	Home	Spouse	Financial income	College education	Purpose in life	Contribution to society
Blood pressure	Get away from self-pity	Autos	Children	Good relationship with boss	Work on additional skills	Increase spiritual awareness	Fun goals
Endurance Energy for physical activity	Get rid of hostility	Saving and investing	Parents	Promotions	Read for personal growth		
Decrease need for medications	Get rid of negative feelings	Vacation	Neighbors	Number one employee	Learn every day		
Increased energy to work on goals	No emptiness	Save for children for college	Fellow humans	Home business			
	No anxiety	Travel around the world	Employee	Retirement			
	Calmness, peace	$$ to help family members					
	Happiness, joy	Life insurance					
	Ability to forgive	Computer					
	Self-derived self-esteem	Other material goals					

way to setting precise and thoughtful goals for the most important aspects of your life.

I. Physical Goals

Am I the proper weight? If not, set a goal of your ideal weight.

What is my physical condition? Make sure you know your blood pressure, cholesterol, blood sugar, and other key measurements of physical condition.

What medications must I take now and how might these be decreased? Anyone on prescription medications for the long-term should be monitored by a physician. Even better, become a partner with your doctor and ask what proactive things you can do to improve your condition and decrease your reliance on medication. Do not ever attempt to reduce dosages without your doctor's instruction, however.

Am I getting enough exercise? Most of us will answer "no" on this one. Set a goal today to become more active and reassess your progress.

Do I have enough physical energy to perform my work easily and still have abundant energy to enjoy life away from my job? Again many of us will say "no." By setting goals in all areas and adhering to them, you will in time restore your physical vitality. We explore further how to improve your energy and health in Chapter 17.

II. Emotional Goals

Do I feel joyous/happy? Record what makes you feel joyful even if such feelings are fleeting. If you have not felt so in a long time, think back to a time when you were very joyous and happy and what made you feel that way.

Am I at peace? Think of the time and conditions when you feel most peaceful and set a goal of recreating this feeling on a regular basis.

Do I feel powerful? Write down what makes you feel powerful and in control of yourself and your life.

Am I invincible? Think of your strengths-how can you build on them to feel truly unbeatable.

Can I forgive? Holding grudges or negative feelings toward people who have let us down doesn't hurt others, only ourselves. Set a goal today to forgive yourself first, and then start forgiving anyone else who may have betrayed or harmed you.

Do I feel energetic emotionally? Often we feel bogged down even when we are in perfect physical health. You can be sure that emotional baggage can and will eventually harm your physical well-being, so set a goal to feel more emotionally energetic. Spend more time with people who are uplifting, and try to inject a feeling of enthusiasm in those who seem to be down all the time.

There is no end to the challenges of realizing emotional well-being, no matter how mentally healthy or aware we are. Think of any area where negative emotions and thoughts are weighing you down, and begin to rid yourself of them. Chapters 9 and 10 describe in detail how to eliminate negative emotions and create a positive emotional state instantly by creating a "new song." **Negative or disempowering emotions can be anger, hostility, depression, anxiety, panic, fear, phobias, hopelessness, worthlessness, inner emptiness, boredom, and feelings of betrayal.**

III. Financial Goals

Financial goals will add to your peace of mind and give you the material tools you require to live and enjoy your life. Getting all financial areas under control will naturally enhance your emotional health, so do give each concept careful consideration no matter how small it may seem.

Do I own my house? Many of us live in a house or apartment which we do not own. If you are not satisfied with your current residence set a goal to acquire your dream home in a specified number of months or years.

Do I have the right kind of car or other vehicles? Set a goal to invest in the car or cars that are right for your family.

Do I have enough money in a contingency fund for emergencies?

Take the precaution of saving here first to ensure your survival in the event of ill health, an accident, job loss, or unpredicted crisis.

Are my investments making money? We're often so busy working to make new money some of us don't pay attention to our investments, and this includes the performance of 401K or IRA accounts. The goal is to understand your investments and make changes where the performance is not satisfactory.

Can I send my children to college? If you have children, one of your goals will be to send them to college or further training after high school. This will require saving more, looking into scholarships and work/study programs, as well as helping the children earn top grades and test scores today.

How will I take care of my parents? With life spans increasing, most of us will be in the position to assist one or both of our parents. How can we do so if we're just making our own expenses? Your parents will have some income entitlements and possibly some of their own assets. Your goal could well be to provide a comfortable life for my parent(s). Understand their finances and your own cash flow, and plan with them today for their future needs.

If I die, will my family have enough resources to carry on without me? Most employers offer life insurance programs, but if you must buy on the open market do so when you are relatively young and healthy-it gets more and more expensive as you age and have health problems. Also plan your estate so your heirs will not have to pay unnecessary taxes. Plan your estate so that the people you love most will benefit from your assets and insurance.

Do we have enough medical/health insurance coverage? Often we hear of families landing in bankruptcy court because of medical bills. This is outrageous and unfair, but a fact of life in America. Set your goal to have comprehensive health and medical insurance coverage so that no matter what befalls your family health wise, your assets and future will be protected.

Do I have a home computer? What was once a luxury item is becoming more and more of a necessity. The benefits of having a home computer increase month by month. They are invaluable tools for research, correspondence, job-hunting, and can save hundreds of dollars each year on long distance communications. The future uses of home computers are limitless, and if you aspire to a home-based business the computer will be the centerpiece of your office and records management. Understanding technology and computing will help you in any future career or business venture. Make a goal to learn about personal computers, find the best one within your budget, and get up to speed on technology.

What specific material goals do I have for myself and/or my family? There will be specific material goals in your family: a vacation home, travel, boat, motorcycle, off-road vehicles, swimming pool, formal gardens . . . create written goals for every need or desire in your family.

IV. Relationship Goals

Do I want to be single for the rest of my life? If you are single and interested in marriage or a permanent relationship, you should set a goal of finding the right partner. This is the easiest thing to put on the back burner, and years can pass without any progress in finding true love. Many wonderful prospective partners exist for every single person, but it takes time and effort to find the best match. If you are single, consider making it your goal to find the right partner and become engaged this year.

Am I giving my spouse enough love and attention? There are so many demands on modern couples that sometimes stable relationships get taken for granted. We grow content and complacent in our marital relationship, and sometimes fail to keep stoking the fires of passion. This mistake can hurt our spouses and make a boring marriage. Just making one night special each week for your spouse can add a lot of spice to your relationship. People spend more time planning a wedding than a successful, fulfilling marriage. Use your imagination and see how happy both of you will be. Make goals to keep your marriage exciting by arranging something special for your spouse one night each week and create variations in your marriage to keep it exciting and interesting.

Am I giving enough time to my child(ren)? In the United States we often have busy work schedules and have very little time left over; the result is that we have more money than we have time available for our children. The tendency in our culture is to give our children material items rather than giving them our time. Your children can have hundreds of dollars worth of toys, clothes, and sports equipment and yet if they do not see you regularly and spend time in activities with you, they do not necessarily develop a sense of your love for them. Make a goal to regularly spend time with your child or children, possibly developing a hobby or some continuing interest together.

What else can I do for my parent(s)? People live longer today but too often those long lives are lonely and less than joyful. Our parents gave us life and raised us to the best of their abilities. No matter how much we visit or help them as they age, there is always more that can be done. Perhaps your parents can take care of themselves, but need to see more of you; maybe your mom or dad is widowed and at a point in life where he or she would like to live with your family; or perhaps frailty has set in and your parent needs a more structured living environment. Consider a goal to take care of your parent(s) forever and see that they are never lonely or discontent.

Are my siblings making it as well as I am in life? In many families one child will exceed all expectations and surpass the achievements of others. If you are doing well financially and your brother or sister is struggling, think of ways you can help them. Could a sibling play a role in your company for part-time income or for a total career change? If they are having trouble getting their first home, can you help with a down payment or help them secure a mortgage? Maybe all they need is moral support and a better approach to life-as you learn, share with them. Make it your goal to help your siblings be as successful and happy as you are.

Am I a good neighbor? It's not unusual to stay so busy that you might not know your neighbors on either side in huge metropolitan areas. In rural areas and small towns this happens as well, but not as often. It pays to be involved in community affairs. Make it your goal to meet your neighbors, offer a helping hand, and become a citizen of your community.

How can I be a better boss or a better employee? If you own the company or run the division, there is more to good management than an adequate compensation package. A pat on the back and a sincere compliment will be greatly appreciated by your staff. Thinking of new ways to improve performance and company productivity will give you a sense of satisfaction as well as a possible promotion. A worthwhile goal is to be sensitive to your employees' contributions to the company and their worth as individual human beings. If you are an employee, your goal could be to make an outstanding contribution to the company that takes care of you, your family, and your future.

What can I do for humanity? This concept may seem abstract and out of reach, but each one of us has a unique talent to serve our fellow man. Think of things that have happened in your life-perhaps terribly painful events-something you had to struggle to overcome. This could be surviving war and actual combat, the suicide of a loved one, suffering and getting out of an abusive relationship, a divorce, bankruptcy-so many tragic events befall us. Those of us who survive have special empathy to those still suffering. If you have been lucky and endured little tragedy in life, you may choose to support the arts, education, literacy-there are hundreds of worthy non-profit organizations that need your time and resources. Make a goal to contribute your special talents to humanity.

V. Employment/Business Goals

Do I have the right job? Your goal might be to find and keep the best job available to you at this time in this marketplace.

How can I increase my income? Remember that what you keep is more important than what you make in the income-producing years. It is natural for everyone to want to keep advancing in earnings as the years go by, but you can also improve your net worth and cash flow by being more conservative in spending. *The happiest people live just below their means-the least happy live above their means.* Make a goal to be creative and develop a new income stream.

How can I get that promotion? Often additional income is right in front of us with our current employer-we just do not have the vision or imagination to make the situation work for us. Your goal may well be to increase your employer's bottom line and become so valuable you will receive a promotion or better pay.

VI. Educational Goals

Do I have enough formal education? For many who married early or had to help support their families, the answer is no. A female bank manager worked her way up to the top position in a regional bank, knew everything that could be known about her company's methods, and took industry training whenever offered. She was a professional, but she was earning 30 percent less than a bank manager across town. This was not a discriminatory action but a matter of education. Starting as a teller in her late teens, the female bank manager has risen slowly through the ranks, while the man across town stayed in school for five years before beginning his banking career. It is easy to argue that the same job should result in the same pay, but it is logical for an employer to offer less to a non-degreed person. In order to get the top pay, you must have the top credentials, and like it or not this means sorting out your formal education. One or two courses per term pass quickly and many colleges now offer credit for life experience. Your goal should be to get a degree in your field of expertise, and seek assistance from your employer and an institution of higher learning to do so.

Do I need a degree for my profession? Many careers require trade school or actual experience, with no specific degree, but all require know-how. If you are working in a dead-end job, explore the opportunities to train for better paying work. A single mother who was working at Wal-Mart stopped into a temporary service one night and was disheartened to learn that she could not pass any of the tests for office/clerical employees. The firm offered free training on word processing and other computer-related skills, and a year later the woman had doubled her salary and improved her lifestyle and self-esteem. This education cost her nothing but her own initiative, time, and commitment. Laborers seeking to work as carpenters, plumbers, or brick-layers, and computer users who like to tinker, can easily prepare for A+ certifications that will enable them to work as well-paid technicians. There are many non-degree tests and certification programs that can change your professional life in a short space of time.

It seems the more schooled we are the more we realize how much more there is to learn. The professions require continuing education, and more and more careers have industry specific courses and exams to keep us on top of new developments and technologies. Your goal might be to stay abreast of the latest advancements in your profession, attend special conferences with your peers, and earn continuing education units to support your formal education.

Magazines, the Internet, and educational television programs provide good information, albeit not in an in-depth form. Your goal should be to read more, especially books that will help you grow as a human being and succeed in life.

VII. Spiritual/Life Philosophy Goals

If you took Psychology 101 in college you already know about the great humanist Abraham Maslow's hierarchy of needs. In Chapter 3 you will learn about Actions for Success and find a detailed discussion of human needs, with an expanded approach. To get you thinking, here is a brief description of the original pyramid:

1. Physiological needs. These needs are biological and consist of the need for oxygen, food, water, and a relatively constant body temperature. These needs are the strongest because if deprived, the person would die.

2. Safety needs. Children often display signs of insecurity and their need to be safe. On the other hand, except in times of emergency or periods of disorganization in the social structure (such as widespread rioting) adults do not experience security needs. There is an expanded view of this need in Chapter 3.

3. Love, affection and belonging needs. People have the need to escape feelings of loneliness and alienation and give (and receive) love, affection and the sense of belonging.

4. Esteem needs. People need a stable, firmly based, high level of self-respect, and respect from others in order to feel satisfied, self-confident, and valuable. If these needs are not met, the person feels inferior, weak, helpless, and worthless.

5. Self-actualization needs. Maslow describes self-actualization as a person's need to be and do that which the person was born to do. It is his "calling." A musician must make music, an artist must paint, and a poet must write. If these needs are not met, the person feels restless, on edge, tense, and lacking something. Lower needs on the scale that are unmet may also produce a restless feeling, but here is it much easier to find the cause.

If we add another side to this pyramid of needs which can transcend all the levels, it would be where true spirituality and philosophical awareness resides. Only a very few individuals do great works for humanity and the planet, turning their backs on material comforts and any trappings of success; one does not have to be a Mother Teresa to serve fellow human beings. Many contribute selflessly to the well-being of others with no thought of repayment, such as a young man I know who runs errands and performs handyman chores for the elderly in his neighborhood.

HITTING THE BULL'S-EYE EVERY TIME

This book is not about theology and supports no specific religion or philosophy; it encourages all readers to understand why they believe what they do and to continue searching for transcendence.

Step 2 – Goals must be precise. If you want to hit the bull's-eye, you need a clearly marked target. For instance, if you write, "My goal is to lose weight," this is far too vague and easily thwarted. However, if you write, "I will weigh 150 pounds," this goal provides a specific target. Here are some examples of vague, easily thwarted goals:

★ *My goal is to have stamina.*
★ *My goal is to have more energy.*
★ *My goal is to be rich.*

To make them targeted, precise, and easily supported goals, change them as follows:

★ *I will be able to run two miles in 16 minutes without feeling exhausted.*
★ *I will be able to spend time with my family after work without collapsing in front of the TV.*
★ *I will make $300,000 by working full-time and creating a new business.*
★ *If you want to hit the bull's eye, you need a precisely marked target, written down in detail, defining each goal. It must be precise.*

Step 3 – Set deadlines. Without a deadline all goals are easily thwarted and discarded. The precision of goals must include time frames and a deadline wherever possible. Write down how many days, weeks, months, or years it will take you to achieve your goals. See how that will improve the goals in Step 2 even further:

★ *I will be able to run two miles in 16 minutes without feeling exhausted* **in two months' time.**
★ *I will be able to spend time with my family after work without collapsing in front of the TV* **by the start of next month.**
★ *I will reduce from 180 pounds to 145 pounds in ten months' time,* **by this date_____.**

★ *I will be out of debt **within three months**.*
★ *I will make $300,000 **in the next two years** by keeping my full-time job and expanding our family business in the evenings and on weekends.*

Step 4 – Why I must achieve this goal. There are many reasons behind every goal we set for ourselves. You need to have the right state of mind to achieve inspiring goals. Writing down all the reasons why the goal must be achieved will reinforce your determination to realize it successfully. For instance, in this example, my goal is:

I will weigh 145 pounds by December 15, 1999.

Think of every reason why you must realize this goal and write them down.

1. I will be healthier.
2. I will be more attractive.
3. I will have more energy.

Then think of the positive results of achieving the goal and add those to your page.

1. If my body is healthy I will live longer, achieve more, have more time to spend time with those I love, and enjoy the extra years of my life in vibrant health. By being lighter, my joints and back will not hurt as much, and it may be possible to decrease the medications I am taking. I'll have fewer doctors' visits and prescriptions, more time, and will save money.
2. If I am more attractive, my partner will want to work harder to be in good shape and we will positively influence our children and others to embrace a healthy lifestyle.
3. If I have more energy I can spend good quality time pursuing sports and recreation with my spouse or children. With more energy I can help my neighbors with chores and my fellow human beings with extra service on committees and in service organizations. I will be more productive at work and contribute more to the success of our company or organization.

Step 5 – **Keep your goal in sight and visualize your goals daily as if they are becoming reality**- Write down your target; look at it every night before bed and every morning when you awaken. People who make New Year's resolutions don't typically write them down, much less keep them in constant sight. **Imagine having this target to remind you each morning and every night:**

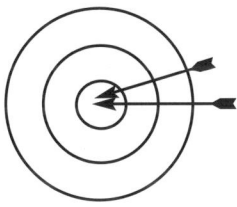

Now imagine having no target – can you see what you are aiming for? ————————> **?**

The darts in the center keep your goals in clear view. The number of pounds and dates on each ring of the target further reinforce how much and when you are to weigh a certain amount until reaching the bull's-eye of 145 pounds-your lifetime goal.

Keeping your goal in sight and realizing you have not yet achieved it causes dissatisfaction, pressure, pain, and will push you to take action. Another method is to put a photograph of a person with the figure you desire on your bathroom mirror where you dress for work each morning. As you look at your own image in the mirror, you will feel pushed and encouraged to look fit and trim. Under the photo write **"I will look like this by December 15, 1999."**

Ask yourself questions each time you take an action, even simple activities like eating, sleeping, and watching television. **"Is this action supporting my goal?"** If you answer "yes" then continue with the activity. If you must answer "no" then the action is thwarting your goal and must be discontinued. For example, if your goal is to lose weight and it is your conditioned response to watch excessive TV while sitting down with beer and potato chips, you will be continually thwarting your goal. If you stop to ask the question before starting to watch TV, you can alter your action and take a half-hour walk in the fresh air, walk on a treadmill, practice yoga or stretching exercises-any useful and supportive activity.

If you find yourself sleeping excessively, ask this question, "Is this action taking me toward my goal of losing weight?" Your brain will answer, "No, of course not!" and there is your cue to cancel this course of action. If you are taking a long walk ask yourself, "Is this action taking me toward my goal?" Your brain will answer, "Yes!" and you can continue with a renewed spring in your step.

<u>Step 6</u> – **Role models, wheels and recipes.** Eating less and exercising more is the only way to lifetime fitness, so we should use periods of weight loss as an opportunity to develop good habits (conditioned responses) for life. If we do not, we are doomed to experience the yo-yo effect and put the weight back on. Don't reinvent the wheel! While Fergie, the Duchess of York, is a good spokeswoman for Weight Watchers, your best friend may be more effective. Find a relative or friend who has lost weight and kept it off for many years. Use that person as your role model, and start off on their set of wheels. Find out what recipe he or she used and follow it exactly without alteration. You need not spend a dime on special dieting programs, because all the research exists on the Internet, in your doctor's office, and in the public library. Most of the problems of mankind are not new. There is someone who has invented a set of wheels or mastered a recipe to get where you want to be. Think of people who have overcome the worst physical or psychological trauma and emerged

HITTING THE BULL'S-EYE EVERY TIME

without disabling mental problems. I guarantee that for any problem you can come up with, there is someone somewhere in the world who, has tackled it, beaten it, and surged ahead with his or her life! Get help from others who have achieved similar goals.

DO NOT REINVENT THE WHEEL!

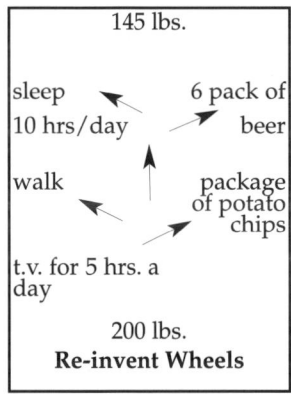

145 lbs.	145 lbs.
sleep 10 hrs/day, 6 pack of beer, walk, package of potato chips, t.v. for 5 hrs. a day	watch caloric intake, eat healthy food, exercise daily
200 lbs. **Re-invent Wheels**	200 lbs. **Role Model**
You are reaching your goal by trial and error. This will take more time.	You will save time and quicken the process to reach your goal.

If you are trying to quit smoking, drinking, using drugs, over-eating, or if you want to neutralize other destructive behaviors like anger, promiscuity, depression a support group system is often useful.

Step 7 – *Write down barriers.* No journey is without hazards or obstacles, so you are well-advised to be aware of and prepared for problems that will hamper your progress. If your conditioned response is to sit for long periods in front of the television eating potato chips and drinking cola or beer, you must note this obstacle. Then you must find ways to overcome your habit time after time until a new, positive-conditioned response is created. Don't buy potato chips and colas or beer when you shop. Being aware of your habits and which habits are obstacles is critical to your success.

Step 8 – Link pleasure to positive actions and understand the benefits of achievement. You can begin taking pleasure in all positive actions, which will aid in making them permanent conditioned responses. Link pain to falling into your old pattern of the destructive behaviors. (Chapter 4 demonstrates how to link pain or pleasure to any event or behavior.) Often when we realize a goal through determination, hard work, and no small amount of personal challenges, the achievement creates a ripple effect. You already know the personal benefits of your goal. It is helpful and supportive of your goal to see the big picture and how your achievements benefit the world around you. How will your success benefit your family? Your neighbors? Your fellow employees? The rest of the world?

Step 9 – Information I need to succeed. What skills do I need to acquire or develop to realize my goal? Action is critical to achieving the goal, but before we can act we must be armed with knowledge. Where can I obtain this knowledge quickly and for the least cost? Who can provide me with this information? Public libraries and the Internet are excellent sources of information.

Step10 – It won't happen overnight, but take actions now! While it is possible to change behavior, overcome phobias, and achieve a goal in a short time, you must not feel it will happen at once. Do not wait until your deadline to do something about your goal or you will end up like the college student who tries writing a term paper hours before it is due. You will be under severe stress to perform. But do act and act now because action is the fuel of success! You must develop a relentless, persistent commitment to take action.

Lexus is a good example. This luxury car came on the American market at a time when Mercedes Benz, Audi and BMW dominated the scene. It didn't happen overnight, but with a "relentless pursuit of perfection" (the corporate motto) Lexus continues to take market share from its competitors. Just as Lexus set a seemingly impossible goal that it is realizing month by month, so must you work day after day relentlessly

HITTING THE BULL'S-EYE EVERY TIME

on your goals to succeed. Mr. Honda who started the Honda car company is another great example of how to achieve goals by years of persistence.

<u>Step 11</u> – **Goals should inspire.** The imagination is a powerful tool; if you can visualize success you can realize any goal and succeed. To realize big success you must dream big. Big goals make you reach for the largest potential within yourself as a human being. Here is an example of an "impossible" goal set by the economic/political leaders of Japan. They set out in 1960 to become the world's number one steel-producing nation-this from a nation with no natural resources for iron or coal! They reached that goal within a decade. By the early 1970s they had realized their goal and by end of the decade they were overtaking the world in automobile production. The United States set up a goal to send a man to the moon and a few years later, the whole world watched an American man walking on the moon. This was achieved by the combined efforts of many working on this goal. So much for impossible goals!

<u>Step 12</u> – **Do not share your goals with others.** Some people don't share their goals for fear of "jinxing" the outcome, but there is a more sensible reason to keep your goals private. Without meaning any harm, others will hear your plans and begin at once to tell you all the reasons why you should not try. They are trapped in the old conditioned response that promotes fear and sees goals, especially ambitious ones, as impossible dreams. Another reason not to share your goals is to avoid competition. If you tell your co-worker it is your goal to become the number one employee and producer in your company, it will be natural for him to step up his efforts or to thwart yours. Share your goals only with those closest to you or those with the same belief/success system. You may share certain goals with others who may remind you of your goals; e.g., losing weight, quitting smoking, etc.

IN SUMMARY – You must be committed to your goals. Keep your eye on the target daily, and reevaluate your goals monthly. Get a system, and act on it day after day. Your goal is not to become a success-motivation author or lecturer but to achieve a precise goal by a specific deadline. Taking consistent daily actions toward your goal will produce results.

More than 90 percent of the population does not set precise goals, which may explain why most of the wealth in the world is in the hands of relatively few people. A study was undertaken on the Yale Class Of 1953. Three percent of the graduating class set precise written goals, developed plans to carry them out, and followed the steps similar to those mentioned in this chapter. Ten percent agreed to setting goals but took a rather casual attitude toward them. Twenty years after graduating, the 3 percent who set the precise goals had realized more success in financial and other areas than the other 97 percent combined. This example tells us that goals are necessary, but follow through-day after day and year after year-makes all the difference.

We have enormous potential to change the world, and with the technological advances in communications we have more opportunities for true cooperation than ever before. Even the old adversaries, Russia and America, are working together on space programs. Once you make the decision to succeed in body, mind, and soul you will be attractive to and attracted by people of like mind. In your nuclear family unit, if husband, wife, and children work together on major goals and simple projects there can be great harmony and progress in the family-rather than wasting time and energy on conflict.

The filter for setting up goals for ultimate success and happiness can be built within yourself. My audiences have commented that this is one of the most powerful tools I have given them. Whenever you set a goal, ask yourself the questions that are listed in Chapter 3 to determine if it is a goal which will create happiness when realized.

You cannot fail if you are meticulous in the pursuit of your goals. Whatever mess you find yourself in life did not happen by accident. Somewhere in your life choices were made to get you where you are now. Did you become overweight by accident? Do you eat chocolate, burgers, fries, ice cream, and chips accidentally? What about watching television for hours and days at a time, is this accidental? Or drinking? Or taking drugs? What about running up huge credit card bills you can't pay? All these destructive activities are done by choice and over time become conditioned responses (habits).

Many people take better care of their cars, dogs, horses, and property than their own bodies; eating excessively, smoking, drinking, and failing to exercise. Likewise, concerned parents establish elaborate goals for their children but none for themselves thinking it "too late" or impossible to succeed in middle age. If you find yourself in this category it is no doubt because of fear, which someone said is, False Evidence Appears Real. We collect this false evidence in our heads, and continually tell ourselves things are impossible. Once your brain has associated fear with a goal, it will automatically collect data to support failure. Chapter 15 will teach you how to get rid of destructive beliefs of fear or failure.

Had Mahatma Gandhi given in to a cultural fear of the British, India would never have won independence. Had Martin Luther King, Jr. given in to prejudice and fear of an America dominated by white men, civil rights and racial equality would never have come to the forefront. If Roger Bannister had given in to the physiological wisdom of his day he would never have been able to run the four-minute mile. Had Madam Curie feared working in a man's world and believed that a woman's place was in the home, radium may not have been discovered for many years.

Somehow these people found the key to success which was within them. It did not come from an outside source. Physically speaking they were the same as you and me and they had the same twenty-four hours of time in a day. We have the potential to dream great dreams and realize great deeds, but we have just as much potential to thwart all our positive actions because of the psyche's propensity to develop negative evidence to support our fears. Our brains can make or break us, and to reprogram them to make us successful we must become aware of the fear/support scenario.

Poverty, physical limitations, and even the horrors of war can be overcome. Many holocaust survivors excelled in the sciences, business, or the arts after years of physical and psychological torture and being dispossessed in some cases of the wealth of several generations. If your background is limited economically, culturally, socially or by any factor, you will need to find a supportive group of people who will help you succeed. There are many success systems which can help you, including those of Deepak Chopra, Anthony Robbins, John Gray and many more. Sometimes the best example to lift you up may be a colleague, teacher, minister, or neighbor who overcame great obstacles to enjoy a comfortable life. It may have looked like your neighbor was born to fail due to the failure of his or her ancestors, but your neighbor made it and so can you.

Remember, without a target to shoot at, without a goal to achieve, you cannot aim high in life; without commitment you cannot achieve success.

Chapter 3

Actions for Success

No matter what culture you come from, no matter where you are born, no matter what language you speak, you have seven basic human requirements. It doesn't matter if you are the president of the United States or Saddam Hussein. It doesn't matter if you are a thief or a preacher; you still have these basic human requirements. Abraham Maslow described a hierarchical organization of needs/requirements for every individual.i He identified a broad range of needs which he regarded as intrinsic and present in everyone and thus labeled them as basic and instinctual. The most essential requirements are survival-oriented requirements, such as food, water, and shelter which he called the D-needs. Only after the D-needs are filled can an individual focus on growth-oriented B-needs or meta-needs. When people meet these requirements they are on the first step of a pyramid toward self-actualization. To satisfy life to the fullest and to create ultimate joy and happiness one must meet many more complex needs, and it is essential to meet these requirements in a healthy way by taking actions beneficial to all of us.

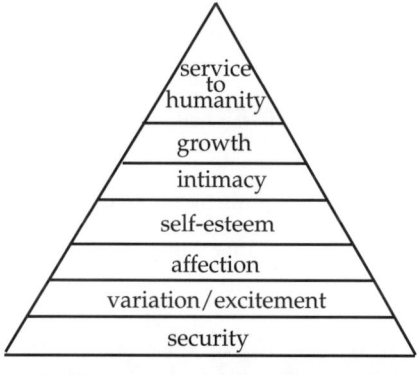

HEMANT THAKUR, MD

SEVEN HUMAN REQUIREMENTS

1. Physiological/Security. The first human requirement is having the funds for food, water, and shelter, and to pay basic bills. This provides the safety and security of our physical well-being. It doesn't matter if you are a football player or a laborer, a street gangster or a teacher, a physician or a call girl, you still need to meet the requirements of having food, water, shelter, and safety. Whether you are born in the wilderness or live in a palace, you still require a roof over your head, water, food and safety. Even when man lived in caves, he was looking for these basic needs for his family. Most people struggle to make this first human requirement all their lives. Just imagine if you are faced with a disaster like a flood, earthquake, or fire, and have no access to water, food, or shelter. How would you feel? Imagine how you would feel if you lost your job or way of earning a living. Without a doubt you would feel insecure and unsafe.

2. Variation/Excitement. I have taken the first two rungs of Maslow's ladder and combined them into the paragraph above so that I could add a second human requirement of variation/excitement. This is the need which, when fulfilled, creates enjoyment in our lives. Why do we watch movies? Why do we attend sports events? Why do we watch soap operas? Why do we travel? Why do people go rock climbing or sky diving? Why do people go canoeing or picnicking? Why do we go to parks? Why do we visit friends? All of these activities create variation and excitement in our lives. Would you watch a movie or a sports event if you knew exactly what was going to happen? Would you play cards or a game of chess if the results were predetermined? If you knew what was going to happen in any game, event or movie, it would be thoroughly boring. We visit friends and travel because it breaks the monotony of routine life.

Often people engage in activities to create variation or excitement in their lives not knowing that those activities may become destructive to themselves and others. For example, people may drink alcohol or take drugs to create excitement in their lives and variation in how they feel. Doing these kinds of activities can be destructive to themselves and others. Another example is when a man, finding his marriage to be routine and perhaps a bit boring, decides to create excitement by having an extramarital affair. Unknowingly, his approach can easily lead him and his family to disaster. If he understands this need, he can furnish excitement in his life by creating a romantic, passionate relationship at home.

Many times commercials are geared toward linking excitement to buying a product or service. We all have this need to create variation in our lives. The Romans had chariot races and gladiators' fighting in order to create excitement; some farmers in Kansas go to rodeo shows for excitement in their lives, and many people go to bars on the weekend looking for excitement. People spend hours at a time watching movies and TV shows, and most people enjoy sightseeing, having a picnic in the park, or visiting interesting places like Disney World, Magic Mountain or Epcot Center. All these meet the second human requirement of creating variation or excitement in our lives. **Uncertainty about what is going to happen also helps us to look forward to the future and be creative.**

3. Affection/Connection. The next human requirement is feeling affection or connection to a loved one or others, such as love for and a relationship with: a) a spouse and children; b) other family members and friends; c) pets like a cat, dog or horse; d) a club, organization, or church; and e) nature and the universe.

One connection we have all experienced is a connection to nature. When we go to church on Sunday morning it provides a sense of connection to a group of people. When we return home and spend time with the family, it gives us a sense of being connected to family members. When you are in love, you feel connected to your lover. When you spend time with your pets like cats, dogs, and horses, you respond to their needs and appreciation for you just as you are. When you join a bird-watching club or a Vietnam veterans' organization you feel connected to that organization. Have you noticed that when you go out for a walk in the park, mountains, wilderness, on the beach by the ocean, streams, or lakes, you feel a sense of peace and connectedness? This may be related to feeling connected to nature. Most people will agree that they feel at peace in one of the natural surroundings.

4. Significance/Self-Esteem. The fourth human requirement is feeling significant, and we all have this requirement. We want to be significant to the people around us. For example when I introduce myself as "Dr. Thakur," I may be trying to gain significance by using the title Doctor. If I introduced myself as a preacher or a chaplain, I will distinguish myself and gain significance as a man of God. If I am the president of a country, it puts me in a position of power and hence significance. What if I am Saddam Hussein, and I want to take over a neighboring country? It makes me significant suddenly all over the world. Man has used violence to be instantaneously significant throughout the history of mankind. It is so easy to gain significance by using violence. All you require is a gun or some sort of weapon. The recent example of killings by teenagers in Columbine High School in Colorado is a vivid example of using violence to gain significance. If teenagers are taught how they can gain significance by what I call Actions for Success or Actions for Improvement, we may prevent these tragedies in the future. A teenager from Australia who read this chapter said, "I wish they would teach us why we do these activities. This book clearly illustrates that we do it to gain significance and meet our human needs. If they would teach us these concepts in school, we would not be getting into trouble and exhibiting odd behavior to gain significance or affection."

If I dress like a biker with big tattoos on my arms and have long hair, I may make people feel wary and gain significance through their fear or my own feeling of being unique. I have personal experience meeting with people from all walks of life and understanding how they

ACTIONS FOR SUCCESS

were trying to feel significant in various ways. If a woman dresses in skimpy clothes with lots of makeup, she is trying to be significant to others through her appearance. When I get involved in a relationship, I want to be significant to my loved one and make her feel significant. People try to gain significance by being a family man, a doctor, a lawyer, a preacher, a gangster, the president, or somebody who gets attention.

Most of us struggle to meet our first four human requirements. I am going to give you a comparison of a family man and a prostitute, and how they are both trying to meet their first four human requirements by their actions.

If I am a family man and I go to church on Sunday mornings, doing these activities helps me to meet my first four human requirements. When I go to church I am sure I am in a safe place where I will meet people with a similar belief system. Being in church exposes me to meeting new people and by attending church picnics or other activities, I have created some variation in my life. There are always new activities for new people who join any church. When I go to church, I am connected to other church members. I am also significant to others when I introduce myself as a family man with my family. I derive self-esteem from being a church member.

Let us look at the second example of a prostitute working in a striptease bar. This person has an income coming in to pay her rent, buy food, and pay bills, thus meeting the first human requirement of security. When she works as a prostitute, it makes her significant to the people around her and creates excitement in her life, thus meeting the second and fourth requirements. Working in the striptease bar makes her feel connected to her co-workers and the people in the bar, and meets her third human requirement of connection. When she dances, it makes her feel significant, as people are sure to pay attention to her and she therefore again meets the fourth human requirement of significance.

Thus the family man and the prostitute who works in a striptease bar are both striving to meet four basic human requirements, but through drastically different modes of action. Many times people do destructive things but they are simply trying to meet basic human requirements.

5. Sexual Intimacy. Even though some cultures have tabooed sex, it is essential for us to have fulfilling sexual intimacy. Think about how many love-stories have been written, and how many movies are made describing sexual intimacy. It does not matter whether you are a president or a preacher, a prince or a servant; it is essential for you to have a good sexual relationship. Kings and queens have fought wars to have the partner of their dreams with whom they felt extremely intimate. People have gone to any length to capture the most intimate relationship. One can go back centuries to the Kama Sutra (the art of making love) or read numerous current magazines, all of which focus on having a wonderful and intimate sexual relationship. Sexual intimacy as an inborn requirement naturally comes to us as we enter adult life.

We need to learn to have an intimate sexual relationship through what we call Actions for Success and not through Actions for Disaster. When people do not have a fulfilling intimate sexual relationship at home, they start looking for it outside, leading to disaster. If one works to master an exciting, fulfilling, and truly intimate sexual relationship with one's spouse or monogamous partner, it will help to create a successful relationship as well as create joy and happiness. By looking for this in extramarital relationships or promiscuous sex, there are many disasters which can result-most importantly sexually transmitted diseases or divorce.

People who choose a celibate life should do so in pursuit of some form of transcendence, not merely as a convenience, avoidance of intimacy, or unwillingness to share.

ACTIONS FOR SUCCESS

These above five intrinsic basic needs are similar to what Maslow described as survival-oriented, physiological D-needs. Once you have achieved these, you may focus on growth-related and self-actualization requirements.

6. Expansion/Growth. The sixth human requirement is expansion. We all have the necessity to continue to grow and expand throughout our life. Growth can occur in the areas of a) educational growth; b) financial growth; c) emotional/psychological growth; d) growth in relationships; e) family/children growth, as we all want our families to do better and better; f) physical improvement growth; and g) spiritual growth.

I have asked the following question in seminars many times, "Are you smarter today than fifteen years ago?" Most people reply that they are indeed much smarter today than they were ten or fifteen years ago. If you don't continue to grow you will feel unfulfilled. We all need to continue to grow in many areas of life. Why do people want to buy a newer and better car or a bigger house; send their children to college; or go to college themselves? It is because people want to continue to expand their horizons. I have seen Vietnam veterans, who, when they are cornered by the system, tend to stay stagnant after getting 100 percent service-connected disabilities. Because they are not growing, they feel unsatisfied in their lives and some have gotten more depressed.

7. Service to Humanity. The seventh human requirement is service to humanity. People who are wealthy many times over still feel unfulfilled because they have not met the seventh human requirement. How many wealthy people do you know or have heard of who have everything money can buy but still feel unfulfilled? If you start giving back to society, to humanity, to the planet, you will find the ultimate joy. People who have played a major role in history, whether a religious leader such as Billy Graham or an entertainer organizing aid to farmers such as Woody Nelson, have focused their attention on the seventh human requirement. There is a common thread linking Mahatma Gandhi, Martin Luther King, Jr., Gautama Buddha and Mother Teresa and many other great leaders. They were all focusing on how they could serve humanity. They devoted their lives serving mankind. We are all part of this universe and we are required to share and help each other. If you don't learn to give back to others, you may feel empty or unfulfilled and try to fill this void with alcohol or drug abuse, collecting more material things, or promiscuous sex, etc.

Maslow's chief way of approaching health was through studies of those persons characterized by "self-actualizing creativeness" which he considered a generalized orientation that leads toward health and growth in life.ii Maslow described self-actualization and peak experiences as episodic, brief occurrences in which the person suddenly experiences a powerful, transcendental state of consciousness. In this state the person experiences a sense of heightened noematic clarity and understanding; intense euphoria; appreciation of the holistic, unitive and integrated nature of the universe and one's unity with it; an altered perception of space and time; and ineffability. Such experiences have been recognized in different cultures and periods and have been called many names including mystical experience, transcendental cosmic consciousness, and satori.

Thus we learned that we all have some basic human necessities/requirements. After we meet the first five basic human requirements, then we need to meet other requirements for ultimate fulfillment and joy. Many people feel empty and unfulfilled despite having accumulated great wealth because they have not met their last two human requirements. It is important for us to learn how to meet these human requirements in an empowering way for all of us.

Many people end up doing destructive things to meet their human requirements. The following exercise will help us to understand how to take Actions for Success every time we perform any activity. Anything

ACTIONS FOR SUCCESS

that we do will fall into the following modes of action whether we are having a cup of coffee or a cocktail, sleeping or watching TV, spending time with our families or going to a bar. **Remember, every action creates a reaction. Remember the law of Karma.**

LAW OF ACTIONS AND CONSEQUENCES OF ACTIONS (KARMA) WHAT YOU SOW, SO SHALL YOU REAP.

Every action generates reaction and a force of energy that will return to us in similar but not necessarily in identical ways.iii If you want to create harmony in life, take actions which will create harmony in life. If you take action to harm someone emotionally, physically, or psychologically it will bring harm to you emotionally and physically. If you give love to someone in abundance, you will receive love in abundance. If you want to create joy and happiness, take actions to create joy and happiness. If you want excellent physical health, take actions to create excellent physical health. If you want to create excellent emotions, health, and joy, take actions to create joy in the lives of others, too. If you want to create wealth, take consistent actions to create wealth.

Karma implies actions of mindful selection. All of us have many choices in our actions. One needs to learn to make attentive choices in every action, including simple actions concerning what we eat, how much we sleep, how we spend time with family, friends or in our work, etc. Remember that all of us, including the most successful people, have only twenty-four hours in a day. What makes a difference is what actions we take every minute. The men and women who become most successful spend most of their time in Actions for Success or improvement, instead of wasting time in watching TV for hours or other nonproductive actions.

As a psychiatrist, I have had the opportunity to counsel thousands of people from all walks of life from firefighters to preachers, homebuilders to executives. It has been a humbling learning experience for me personally to have worked with people who suffer tremendously in many ways: physically, spiritually, financially, legally, and in their family relationships,. We all would do well to remember this: **Whatever is happening at the current minute is a culmination of all the decisions you made in the past.**

I have seen numerous people make the choice of hanging around with friends or acquaintances who are betraying others, and then make conscious choices to betray others and become treacherous themselves. Then they get furious when they find themselves betrayed. They also create anxiety for themselves as they live in fear and paranoia of being caught. I saw a woman who was chronically cheating on her husband when he was out of town. She wondered why she was seeing a psychiatrist for chronic anxiety, for which she also used alcohol to calm down. Eventually she got so depressed and anxious she began to take both Alprazolam and an anti-depressant. She failed to tell her psychiatrist all this time that she was cheating on her husband and that she had been drinking to calm herself down. I do not know of any pill which is going to stop the stress people create by these Actions for Disaster. On the other hand, people who bring peace and joy into the lives of others will have peace and joy coming to them. People who help others will have help coming their way. People who care for families will have families caring for them. People who spend time building relationships will have wonderful relationships. Sometimes it may not seem fair, but if we keep taking Actions for Success, eventually all the good we do will return to us.

Most of the time, people take actions due to past conditioned responses without consciously making a choice. Here is a good example: If a man is challenged in a bar, he makes an unconscious choice from conditioned responses to get into the fight, in order to prove he is a macho guy. I call this an Action for Disaster. Then he wonders why he has a broken nose and numerous assault charges, head injuries that may cause memory loss, and resulting legal and financial problems. On the

ACTIONS FOR SUCCESS

other hand, I met a martial arts expert who always chose to take what I call Action for Success. He always managed to walk away from fights without hurting others or getting hurt himself.

Another example is people living a **TGIF** (Thank God it's Friday) life, because their minds have been conditioned to live for the weekend. Someone has linked in their brains that the meaning of pleasure is partying-that they can enjoy themselves only when they are not working. Naturally such people find it very difficult to get up the motivation to work long hours, start or operate a business, and really become successful. If they learn to make a conscious choice of taking Actions for Success, they will save themselves a bundle of grief, pounds of pills, and numerous visits to a shrink. I met many TGIF believers when I ran an alcohol/drug rehabilitation program, and it is sad to see lives in ruins because of a faulty belief. I have been treating a CEO of a major United States company who has finally sobered up after many years of evening binges of drinking alcohol at bars and clubs. He now realizes what a lie he was telling himself when he was going to bars and sitting there engaged in idle chatter. It is no wonder to him now that he had problems in relationships, problems with depression, and multiple physical problems, including a stroke. He now realizes that his old pattern of going to bars was a conditioned response someone put in his head that this was the only way to socialize. This was not his conscious choice. The person or company who put this conditioned response in his head either wanted to make a buck in promotion of a harmful lifestyle (thereby selling their products) or it may have come from a parent or role model who had been likewise brainwashed. Problems of mankind are created by man, and the solutions to them are within us. In this CEO's case he has now realized he can socialize by using Actions for Success. In simple terms, you reap what you sow, and every action generates a reaction.

It is essential for us to make conscious choices in our actions. Learn to examine your actions to see if they are conditioned responses with disastrous results. For example, if someone curses me, I should examine my choices of how to respond. Most people respond by cursing back or getting into a physical fight due to past conditioned ways of reacting to it. This will create pain and suffering for both parties. If you learn to make a choice of not accepting another's cursing at an emotional level, it will have a powerful result and fall under Actions for Success. I have also seen people with the title of "boss" responding in a conditioned pattern when employees did not obtain their permission at every turn. They refused to realize that employees were trying to do something beneficial for customers and the company.

Empowering Ways of Choosing Actions.

First learn to make a conscious choice in every action instead of falling prey to conditioned responses. Many people, from teenagers to church-going middle-aged audiences in my seminars have commented that the following system is a very powerful tool to use in scanning their choices before taking action. Before you take any actions, ask the following questions:

1. What will be the end result of this choice/decision for me? Will this choice/decision bring joy to me?
2. What will be the result of this choice for my family and will it bring happiness to them? (I recently heard a radio commercial asking listeners to ask this question while making any choice).
3. What would be the consequences of this choice to my neighbors and fellow human beings? Will this choice bring happiness to fellow human beings?
4. Does this choice serve all mankind and humanity? Is this choice beneficial to the planet? (This is what Gautama Buddha, Mahatma Gandhi, Mother Theresa focused on).
5. How do I feel in my heart, and how does my conscience feel? If it causes even the faintest discomfort or uneasiness, do not take that

ACTIONS FOR SUCCESS

action and re-examine the situation. Learn to pay attention to your gut feeling and your bodily sensations.

6. Do I get feelings of pleasure at the thought of this choice?

Laws of Action

These Laws of Action are based upon the laws of the universe.

Six Questions to Ask	Actions for Success	Actions for Improvement	Actions for Disaster	Crazy Actions
Happy consequences to me.	Yes	Yes	No	No
Happy consequences to family.	Yes	Yes	No	No
Happy consequences to fellow humans.	Yes	Yes	No	No
Serve mankind and planet Earth.	Yes	Yes	No	No
Your gut feeling/body sensation.	Comfortable	Comfortable	Uncomfortable	Uncomfortable
Feeling of pleasure.	Yes	No	Yes	No

The universe, or nature, works in perfect harmony, with each action supporting every other action and nurturing every living being while synchronizing zillions of reactions a second. If you master taking the actions which fall into the category of Actions for Success, you are on the path to success. You can use this same chart when evaluating your value and belief system. When you master the evaluation steps for taking Actions for Success and Actions For Improvement out of numerous choices, you are on the path to ultimate success. Make sure every action you take falls into these two categories. One of my patients had a history of violent behavior, had been in prison many times, had abused drugs, was homeless, and was unable to relate to his son and ex-wife. However, when he learned to understand and use this process, he turned his life around in less than twelve months. Now he is going to college, lives in a house, dates a nice woman, and relates well to his son, his ex-wife and his brothers. To top it off, he was able to give a speech to college students based upon the principle of these Laws of Action. Today he tells me and others that he keeps asking himself at every moment the above questions, and checking his actions to see if they fall into the categories of Actions for Success and Actions for Improvement or if they fall into categories of Actions for Disaster or Actions That Are Crazy." He mastered the methods for quickly evaluating actions, which fall into the categories of "Actions for Success" and "Actions for Improvement." It turned his life around. In the past everyone was afraid of him. Today his brother can't believe that this man has changed so much, is going to college, and is a pleasure to be around.

Take actions which nurture you and all of us.

If you want to succeed, master the methods of making conscious choices of every action. **Whether you want to create wealth, a wonderful relationship, or an abundance of emotional/physical energy, master the ability to take Actions for Success and Actions for Improvement.** If you do so, all good things will start coming to you. As you practice taking Actions for Success and Actions for Improvement, it will become a spontaneous response.

<u>Actions for Success</u>

If the answer is "yes" to all six questions in the quick evaluation, your actions will lead to success. Let us try this by doing a simple exercise. If you are watching excessive TV, your answer is going to be "no" to some of these questions. This is because watching excessive TV will cause inactivity and physical problems, and you are taking away valuable time from your spouse and kids. If you are doing gardening and you ask yourself the questions all your answers will be "yes."

<u>Actions for Improvement</u>

Let us prove this on another example. You plan to lose weight and start exercising every day. Ask the above six questions about the activities of exercise and eating a healthy diet. Your answer to the sixth question, "Do I get feelings of pleasure?" will be "no" at first because your body hurts initially and you may not like the change in diet from eating fried foods to healthy foods. The answer to the other five questions is going to be "yes." If your actions fall into this category, you are on your way to making improvements in your life. Most activities which will lead to improvements in your life like losing weight, creating more physical energy, improving your financial status, and improving your relationships, will all fall into this category. Any initial life changes for improvement may not give pleasurable feelings to you at the beginning.

Actions for Disaster

Ask those six questions again every time you are performing any activity. For example, activities like going to a bar, drinking alcohol, using drugs, smoking, eating excessively, doing excessive shopping, watching excessive TV, carousing in bars, or having extramarital affairs will fall into this category. In this case the answer to your sixth question is going to be "yes" as the activity may feel pleasurable. The answers to the rest of the questions will be "no." Advertisers have a lot of strategies for promoting actions which fall into this category as their only goal is to make a buck. If I sell my beer it may feel pleasurable to be making a lot of money, but I may cause harm to my own family, my neighbor's family, and the rest of the world because of alcohol-related problems. Chapter 4 provides details of how alcohol affects all of us physically, financially, legally, emotionally, in our relationships, spiritually, and in causing destruction in our society.

Actions Which Are Outright Crazy

Ask those six questions again every time you are performing any activity. Joining a gang, abusing drugs, physically hurting others and other actions fall into this category. For example, if a person is robbing somebody at gunpoint it doesn't give him a pleasurable feeling because he knows he will either get arrested or hurt himself or someone else. He knows it may end in the bad consequence of him going to prison. He knows it has bad consequences for his children and wife because when they find out he robbed somebody then he is not a good role model for them. He knows this action has bad consequences for his neighbor as his neighbor doesn't want a bad role model in his neighborhood, and he is certainly not serving mankind/humanity or planet Earth. The answer to all six questions in this case is going to be "no." I had the chance to speak about this to hundreds of prisoners when I worked as a psychiatrist on Riker's Island Prison in New York City.

Just get into the habit of asking these simple questions to yourself every time you perform any action. If your actions fall into the categories of Actions for Success and Actions for Improvement, you are on the path to success. Also use these questions to filter your belief and value system. **If your value system and beliefs fall into the categories of Actions for Success and Actions for Improvement, you are matching the software in your brain to the software of successful people. Remember, do not reinvent the wheel. This will lead you onto the path of ultimate success.**

What do we do with our past Actions of Disaster and Actions Which Are Outright Crazy? Most people continue on the path of Actions of Disaster and continue to cause more suffering to themselves. They are unconsciously paying their "Karmic debt." One cannot change his or her past. I have yet to see anyone who has managed to change the past. I know I cannot change my past. However, you can make use of past Actions of Disaster by giving them an empowering meaning in the present moment. Ask yourself the following questions when you think about your past activities which fell in the category of Actions for Disaster.

1. What can I learn from my past Actions for Disaster?
2. How can I make use of this for the benefit of myself and others?
3. How can I make use of this to help humanity?

Now let us take the example of the above patient who was violent, in and out of prison, doing drugs/alcohol, etc. He asked the above

ACTIONS FOR SUCCESS

questions and came up with the following answers:
1. My past actions caused emotional pain to me and my family. It caused financial loss, loss of relationships, and numerous physical problems. I lost my home and family. My brothers were afraid to talk to me.
2. I have learned that doing these Actions for Disaster and pure crazy actions will cause ultimate pain. I am going to stop taking those kinds of actions. I will take different actions, which fall into the categories of Actions for Success and Actions for Improvement. I will teach my children and others how these Actions for Disaster cause ultimate pain.
3. I will take actions to teach others that alcohol, drugs, or violence do not solve problems. They only create more problems, pain, and suffering in all areas of life.

In fact this man taught a class to other college students based upon these principles. This is the same man who used to be afraid to talk to groups of people in the past. Even though we can not change our past, we can learn something empowering from it and make use of it to benefit ourselves and others.

*Every good thought you think is contributing
its share to the ultimate result of your life.*

(Grenville Kleiser)

---

[i] Harold I. Kaplan, M.D. and Benjamin J. Saddock, M.D., Synopsis of Psychiatry, Behavioral Sciences Clinical Psychiatry. Baltimore: Williams & Wilkins, 1988.
[ii] See note i above.
[iii] Deepak Chopra, The Seven Spiritual Laws of Success. San Rafael, California: Amber Allen Publishing, New World Library, 1993.

Chapter 4

The Two Masters
Driving Human Behavior

As I mentioned earlier there is no point in wasting time reinventing the wheel. It may be best to find a pre-existing set of wheels or a recipe. Here is a recipe someone mastered a long time ago. Thousands of years ago in the sacred Hindu text, **Bhagavad-Gita**, it was written, **"He who masters the pain and pleasure will master it all."**i What this means is that our behavior is driven by trying to avoid some kind of pain and gain some kind of pleasure. However it is up to us to link the meaning of pain and pleasure to any object or event. We will explain later, in this and other chapters, how to link the meaning of pleasure or pain to any event. For most people pain and pleasure govern life. If we learn to govern pain and pleasure, we can conquer whatever challenges we encounter and achieve any objective. If we learn this recipe of controlling the meaning of pain and pleasure, we will be masters of all.

If you go back thousands of years ago to the time of the caveman, you may wonder what drove his behavior to live in a cave, search for food and protect his family. The answer is that he knew he would be in pain if he didn't have enough food and water for himself and his family, and if he didn't protect his family he would be done. So what force was driving his behavior? It was the pain of not having food and water for himself and his family. This pain drove him to go out and hunt for food and search for a cave for his family. Why is it then that in this modern age we live in a house with a nice air conditioner and a heating system? It is because we want to avoid the pain of being cold or hot. Look at any activity that you do throughout the day. The simple activity of going to work is driven by trying to avoid the pain of not having an income to support oneself and the family. We want the money to gain the pleasure of having access to a house in which to live, and to buy items for fun and comfort. What about the activity of watching television? It is related to avoiding the pain of boredom, escaping from daily stresses and having the pleasure of excitement. Let us look at some other activities. We carry pagers and cellular phones and we use microwave ovens. These behaviors are driven by the two forces of gaining pleasure and avoiding discomfort or pain.

I was just talking to a friend of mine from Australia who said, "Hemant, I have to finish this essay for my master's degree. If I procrastinate and do not finish this essay in the next two days, I will be in trouble (in pain) because I will have to retake the course and examination again for which I will be required to pay another $700." So her preparing for her examination is driven by the two masters of avoiding pain and gaining pleasure.

Let me give you another example. A friend of mine waits until the last day (procrastinates) to prepare her tax returns as she feels that preparing a tax return is painful and boring. She has other more pleasurable things to do like watching television, going to the movies and attending parties. However when the deadline comes she suddenly gets up, starts preparing her tax return, and becomes frantic in the process, all because she knows that not submitting the tax return will be even more painful. She has left completing her tax return to the last minute. Why did she wait all these days? She waited because she felt that completing the tax return was painful and boring, and doing something else was more pleasurable. This was until the time came when she realized that if she does not prepare and file the tax return she would have the tremendous pain of paying fines and facing the IRS. Suddenly her brain says, " If you do not finish this tax return you will be in tremendous

THE TWO MASTERS

pain." This forces her to take actions to complete the tax return just before the deadline. We have all done similar things in our life. We put off taking actions or procrastinate about completing a project as we engage in other activities which are perceived as more pleasurable.

Even when we do destructive activities, for example, when we smoke or drink alcohol, we are driven by the intent of avoiding pain and gaining pleasure. At the initial moment when we are doing these activities, we are trying to avoid pain or the discomfort of an uncomfortable state of mind such as anxiety, nervousness, emptiness, anger or being bored. When people don't like the way they feel, when they feel some kind of pain or emptiness, nervousness, or some other uncomfortable feeling; they think that they are going to have some pleasure by taking a smoke or a drink or doing excessive shopping or excessive eating. At that very moment the intention is to avoid pain or discomfort and gain some pleasure. Take the example of someone who is doing street drugs. Just prior to doing cocaine the person feels dysphoric, anxious, and depressed, or some other uncomfortable state of mind. He knows that if he smokes cocaine he would have a sense of pleasure in a matter of minutes. When people do destructive activities like using street drugs or alcohol, eating excessively, smoking, shopping excessively or having promiscuous sex, at the very moment they do the destructive activity, they are trying to avoid pain or an uncomfortable state and gain some pleasure. People often fail to see that on a long-term basis these activities will cause pain. Take any activity you do from the morning to night, and you will discover you do many of these activities, to avoid some pain or discomfort and gain some pleasure.

Let me give you another example of a woman I knew. She was married, but would go to bars and flirt with men, have a few drinks, and end up having sexual relationships with them. From a conversation with her, I learned that when she was young and went to rodeos, she saw men getting drunk and she found the men were fun and pleasurable to be around as they were talkative and funny. They were also approaching women to have sexual liaisons, which she found exciting. In this case the men were giving this woman attention-significance. Thus her brain unknowingly had linked going to a bar and flirting with men as pleasure. Once this was linked in her brain, her behavior was on autopilot. After she grew up and married she continued to seek this pleasure, not realizing the long-term disastrous effects of losing her marriage as well as catching a sexually transmitted disease. At the very moment she took the disastrous action of flirting in the bar, her brain was still trying to avoid pain, boredom, and emptiness, and in so doing to gain pleasure. She failed to realize that continuing these actions (Actions for Disaster as we call them) would ultimately lead to pain. People who smoke, drink excessively, use drugs, eat excessively, shop excessively, or have extramarital relationships do not realize they will have ultimate pain. They are operating on the basis of gaining short-term pleasure. If we want to succeed we need to learn that instead of pain and pleasure governing our behavior we should govern pain and pleasure. Remember that every action generates a reaction, as we have described in Chapter 3.

As a psychiatrist, I have seen thousands of Vietnam veterans. Many of them used alcohol and/or drugs. Most of them said they used alcohol or drugs to numb their emotional pain of sadness, depression, anxiety, panic, fear, anger, and the inability to sleep due to frightening and painful dreams. When they were using drugs and alcohol, their brains were still trying to avoid pain and get some level of comfort. They did not realize that drinking alcohol and using drugs would cause the ultimate pain of losing jobs and families, being sent to prison, and ending up suicidal, homicidal, and in psychiatric wards. Once they learned to deal with their emotional pain in constructive ways, they quit using drugs and alcohol. Many of them now verbalize that they have learned how destructive it was to abuse alcohol or drugs, but did not realize this at the time.

THE TWO MASTERS

The two masters which drive human behavior are pain and pleasure.

The following diagram will illustrate how every activity we do is driven by trying to avoid some kind of pain and gain pleasure. This is one of the most important concepts to learn if we want to manage our lives. By the end of this book you will learn how to link the meaning of pain and pleasure to any event.

The Two Masters Which Drive Human Behavior

Work for a living: Pain of not having food/shelter. If I earn a living I will have the pleasure of food/shelter.

Driving a car: Avoiding the pain of walking. Comfort of traveling fast & pleasure/luxury of auto.

Watch TV/movies: Avoid the pain/discomfort of problems of the day. Gain pleasure of excitement from shows or films.

Travel: Avoid discomfort/boredom of routine. Gain pleasure/excitement of visiting new places.

Eating cheesecake: Avoid boredom of routine. Pleasure of eating sweets.

Getting on Internet: Escape boredom/emptiness. Excitement of meeting someone/visiting new sites.

Visit a friend: Avoid boredom/emptiness. Gain pleasure of companionship/friendship.

More education: Avoid the pain of less income. Pleasure of earning higher income/growth.

Example: People who dislike school may link pain to studying and pleasure to not mastering the effort to study.

Let us now look at some destructive activities or what we call Activities for Disaster. Our intention is to avoid pain and gain pleasure. This, of course, is on a short-term basis.

Drinking alcohol: Avoid pain of boredom/ anxiety/stress/depression/anger/ emptiness/routine.

Extramarital flirting: Avoid boredom in routine/ non-exciting relationship.

Smoking: Avoid pain of boredom/anxiety/ nervousness/stress.

Eating excessively: Avoid pain of boredom/ anxiety/nervousness/stress.

Using street drugs: Avoid pain of boredom/ anxiety/nervousness/stress/depression.

Shopping excessively: Avoid pain of boredom/ nervousness/stress.

Gain pleasure/ excitement of going to bar and flirting / gossiping/socializing.
Gain pleasure of flirt ing/involved in sexual escapade with a new partner.
Gain pleasure of escaping from boredom/anxiety/ nervous feeling.
Gain pleasure of escaping from boredom/anxiety/ nervous feeling.
Gain pleasure of feeling euphoric and escaping from boredom/anxiety/ nervous feeling.
Gain pleasure of escaping from boredom/anxiety/ nervous feeling.

Advertisers successfully link pleasure in our brain to using their product and pain to not using their product. It works most of the time. If you watch any television commercial, you will see how successfully this is done. They have made us believe that you have to have brand name shoes to feel good, you have to drink beer to have fun, you have to shop in a certain shopping center to feel good and have pleasure. You have to smoke to have the pleasure of feeling good or relaxed and to feel that, "You've come a long way, baby." If advertisers can link these meanings in our minds so easily, why don't we link a useful meaning we want in our brain-a meaning which will fall into the category of <u>Actions for Success</u>. Later I will demonstrate how you can link any meaning to any event or object.

So what is it that stops people from taking action? It is still related to linking pain to taking actions and linking pleasure to not taking actions. For example, if I decide to lose weight and improve my physical health, I will have to take the actions of stopping at grocery stores, picking up healthier items like fruit, vegetables, and chicken and take the action of preparing meals. I also have to take the action of making time everyday to exercise regularly. People have linked pleasure in their minds to stopping at fast food joints for a hamburger, french fries, and soda pop and coming home to watch television. They have also linked pain to stopping at the grocery store to pick up healthy food items, preparing meals each day, and taking time to exercise, which may be painful initially. As we have learned by this time, our brains will automatically choose activities to avoid pain and gain pleasure. In this case, our brains will choose the activities of stopping for fast food and coming home to watch television. <u>Unless we master how to link pleasure to stopping at the grocery store, selecting healthy food and preparing healthy meals, and exercising regularly, we will have tremendous difficulty changing our behavior.</u> Later I will teach you how one can link the meaning of pleasure or pain to any event. Usually the meaning of pain and pleasure is linked in our brains unknowingly by advertisers, events occurring in our environment, or people around us.

HEMANT THAKUR, MD

How many drinks in an hour? Number of drinks* it takes to reach alcohol blood levels on an empty stomach.

Impairment: Most drivers are significantly impaired at .08 with driving tasks such as: braking, steering, lane changing, judgment, divided attention.

Blood alcohol level 0.08 / 0.10
Weight / Number of drinks

In other countries: Blood alcohol level to be considered legally drunk:

Weight	0.08	0.10	Country	Level
100 lbs.	2.5	3	Sweden	0.02
120	3	3.75	Finland	0.05
140	3.5	4.25	Netherlands	0.05
160	4	5	Norway	0.05
180	4.5	5.5	Australia	0.05- 0.08
200	5	6.25	Austria	0.08
220	5.5	7	Britain	0.08
240	6	7.5		

One drink* equals 12 oz. can of beer, 5 oz. glass of wine, or one shot of distilled spirits.
**34 states recognize .10 as being legally drunk, 16 states say .08
Sources: National Highway Transportation Safety Board, Illinois Transportation Dept.ii
Alcohol is a central nervous system depressant like other anesthetics. At 0.05 percent level alcohol in blood, thought, judgment, and restraint are loosened and sometimes disrupted.
Many studies indicate that task impairment begins when blood alcohol reaches about 0.05%. iii
Refer to *Modern Synopsis of Psychiatry*, H. Kaplan, M.D. and B. Saddock, M.D. and/or information from **MADD**

Consider another example of a person who drinks excessively. This person may drink because it has been linked in his brain that he will have pleasure if he drinks alcohol-he will have the pleasure of relaxation. Advertisers, peer pressure and habit have systematically done this. People want to be somebody significant and by taking a particular drink, which the advertiser has linked to feelings of significance, you will feel significant, which will give you pleasure. If you stop for happy hour each evening you will encounter your peers and be accepted and again made to feel significant. The following scenario will make this clear. It is done using Pavlovian conditioning and it works on millions of people.

THE TWO MASTERS

1. Want to have **fun with an attractive and sexy blond?** . . . **Drink our beer.**
2. You want to **enjoy a football game?** . . . **Drink our beer.** (Scientific neuropsychological testing studies show that if you have even two or three drinks, your neuropsychological as well as visual/motor perception will be impaired. You will not pick up every detail during visual activities.)
3. You want to **be a tough cowboy?** . . . **Drink our beer.**
4. You want to **be a successful lawyer?** . . . **Have some martinis.**
5. You want to **be lawmaker?** . . . **Have some cocktails.**
6. You want to **have fun?** . . . **Drink our beer.** (The truth is alcohol-related problems cost the people of the United States $128.3 billion in 1986 according to a report to Congressiv, and guess how much more it is costing in 1998? Who is getting rich and who is having fun? Certainly not the people who drink!)
7. You want to **be a family man?** . . . **Have our wine.**
8. You want to **celebrate Thanksgiving or Christmas in style?** . . . **Serve our wine.**
9. Want to have **fun on New Year's Eve?** . . . **Have our champagne.**
10. Want to **relax after a stressful day?** . . . **Drink our liquor.**

Once this is linked in our brain, we respond as if it is real. It is like the conditioned responses of Ivan Pavlov and his dog, or the Vietnam veteran who jumps when the door is slammed. The dog was intentionally trained to salivate at the ringing of the bell and the veteran was unconsciously trained to be hyper-alert to loud noises (which are associated with gunfire). Alcohol manufacturing companies have spent millions of dollars studying how they can link the meaning of pleasure to their products by conditioning. It is easy to condition people's minds and link the meaning of pleasure to any object or event. Ask a Vietnam veteran how his mind was conditioned unknowingly, how he started perceiving it as real and how his brain reacts in few seconds. The following chapter will give details about how we form conditioned responses, many times unknowingly.

Let us analyze how a person who is drinking responds to the pain/pleasure forces.

Pain if I do not drink alcohol
1. Boredom, no date, no socialization.

2. No excitement or variation; boredom.
3. Pain of feeling low, insignificant.

4. Pain of not feeling strong/successful

5. Pain of not getting some recognition/ relaxation
6. Pain of no fun, being bored, feeling empty.
7. Pain related being conditioned to "You have to drink to have a successful celebration." No drinking, no sense of celebration.
8. Pain of facing stress; full day/ being tired.

Pleasure if I drink alcohol
Have fun with an attractive and sexy blond woman.
Enjoy a football game/any sport.
Pleasure of feeling like a tough man or cowboy.
Pleasure of feeling like a successful lawyer.
Pleasure of feeling like a successful lawmaker.
Pleasure/ fun/excitement of party atmosphere.
Pleasure of celebration.

Pleasure of feeling relaxed

Here are the keys to unlock your human emotional chains!

How can we change this? If we link massive amounts of pain to drinking alcohol, our brains will tell us to quit. How can we do this? It can be done in exactly the same way advertisers link pain and pleasure in our brain. Do not reinvent the wheel! Let us use what already works on our brains in a constructive way! There are also additional techniques to maintain sobriety.

THE TWO MASTERS

Let me give you a recipe for changing any destructive or disempowering behavior. James had been a heavy smoker for most of his life and smoked two packs of cigarettes a day. He suddenly stopped smoking overnight. How did he do that? If one can understand the process behind this, you will have a recipe to change any behavior, any belief system, and any value system. James was sitting alone in his apartment. He felt a sudden severe chest pain and could not breathe. He was gasping for air and terrified he was going to die. He reached for the phone and dialed the number 9-1-1 for emergency help. However he could not speak because he was unable to breathe. He was terrified that in a few minutes he was going to die. He realized it had to do with his smoking. Doctors had been telling him he has emphysema from smoking and it would kill him. He was in tremendous pain, gasping for air, trying to speak to the operator to send for some help. He could not speak a word. The operator realized there was something wrong and sent for help by tracking him down by caller ID. Four or five minutes later James heard a knock on the door. He wanted to move but he could not, due to lack of air. The paramedics kicked down the door and entered the apartment to find James turning blue. He was taken to the hospital where he found out he had ruptured emphysematous lung tissue, causing lung collapse. It was due to smoking. He learned from the doctors he would have been dead in another two to three minutes if the paramedics had not arrived. James had a painful near-death experience which was linked to smoking. This incident linked massive pain to smoking in James' mind. He also realized he would have the pleasure of living only if he stopped smoking. James stopped smoking after this incident and never smoked again. He shares his story with other patients now. Let us understand what happened here. There is a very important recipe for changing any behavior in this incident. The terrifying, painful, life-threatening feeling was linked to smoking in James' mind. This stopped his smoking overnight. If we apply this process or recipe to anything we want to change, we can change any destructive or disempowering behavior or any belief system in a short time. We can link the meaning of terrifying pain to destructive or disempowering behavior, and the meaning of pleasure to getting rid of the destructive behavior.

Let us take the example of how we can link pain to drinking alcohol and pleasure to not drinking it by using the above recipe. The following example will illustrate this.

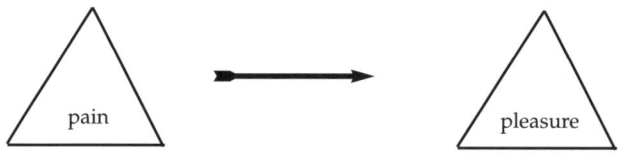

Pain if I drink alcohol.   Pleasure if I do not drink alcohol.

Pain if I drink alcohol: Linking **massive pain** to drinking.

Alcohol affects us physically and causes destructive effects to practically all areas of the body. It affects our brain, causing damage to brain cells, which in turn causes memory loss. This memory loss is caused by the direct toxic effect of alcohol on the brain cells, head injuries from bar fights, or falling down and bumping the head. It causes possible decreased oxygenation to every cell in our body due to blood loss and anemia, which is also caused by alcohol. This will cause the drinker to have decreased functioning and poor job performance. It causes decreased concentration, symptoms of depression, anxiety, paranoia and even hallucinations (in some cases). These symptoms cause many people who drink alcohol to visit psychiatrists, psychologists, and other types of therapists, paying them hundreds of dollars in fees. Who is losing in this process? Any one of the stages of alcohol abuse, including intoxication, cutting down on alcohol and withdrawal symptoms, can cause paranoia and transient hallucinations in some people. Dementia caused by alcohol can induce transient paranoia, and some people develop a condition called "alcohol hallucinosis" which can cause chronic hallucinations even after the person stops drinking, resulting in a need for antipsychotic medications. Think about the devastating effects these symptoms may have on individuals and their families. The answer to their anxiety, nervousness, depression, and paranoia is medications which will cost them more money and have some side effects. Who is the loser again? The person who is drinking is the loser and having pain. Who is making money? The alcohol distillers and pharmaceutical companies and related industries are having the pleasure of making money and having fun. Some alcoholics can develop transient, severe, alcohol-induced dysphoric mood disorder when they feel intensely depressed, suicidal, and hopeless. I have seen this in the Emergency Room many times. A man was presented to the Emergency Room with suicidal depression while intoxicated. The next day I saw him and he was feeling fine. However, during his periods of intense dysphoria he had wanted to kill himself by jumping off a bridge on an interstate highway. Fortunately, he was stopped in time by the police. You cannot wake up a dead man and say, "You made a mistake," and give him a second chance! (By the way, this was transient dysphoria caused by alcohol and not clinical major depression.) One needs to realize that when this young man dies, his wife and children are going to suffer for many years due to the loss of his companionship and naturally they'll experience financial problems. As a psychiatrist, I have seen this scenario hundreds of times. Alcohol can transiently induce almost any psychiatric symptom.

Alcohol can cause facial injuries from bar fights, being beaten up by others, and premature aging due to decreased oxygenation and poor nutrition. Remember that every cell in the body needs oxygen and nutrition to function properly. Facial injuries and scars may cause poor self-esteem in some. Many alcoholics have broken noses due to falling down on their faces and being in fights.

Alcohol is an irritant to the gastrointestinal tract. Chronic use of alcohol can cause ulcer disease in the upper gastrointestinal tract. Ulcer diseases can cause silent bleeding and blood loss, resulting in anemia. It can also cause malabsorption syndrome due to the toxic effects of alcohol on the intestinal and stomach lining. I have seen some patients who drink experience a drop in their hemoglobin level of seven to eight grams, and they are not even aware of it. Combining anemia caused by blood loss, poor nutrition, and poor eating habits will cause decreased oxygenation in the body as the oxygen carrying capacity is decreased due to less hemoglobin. Decreased oxygenation will cause cellular deterioration in every cell in the body, causing the symptoms of fatigue, tiredness, a lack of energy and aging at the cellular level, including the skin and every organ in the body. When one is tired, he cannot help his family, nor do his job properly.

Now visualize someone with the symptoms of a pain in his or her stomach, or gastrointestinal upset. What will this person do? He will end up going to a doctor, which will cost him or the insurance company, causing everyone else's insurance rate go up. If this person does not have insurance, the taxpayer will have to pay his bills through Medicare or Medicaid. I have seen some indigent alcoholics who were hospitalized in a state hospital and their hospital bills came to thousands of dollars. Who pays these bills? The taxpayers, which include most of us. After he is examined, he will be asked to come back for another test called a gastroscopy. He will be sedated and examined by a camera, which is passed down his esophagus into his stomach, at the cost of a few hundred dollars more. Think about who is experiencing the discomfort of the procedure, losing money and time, and who is getting rich.

This is just the beginning of his problems. After he is shown pictures of holes (ulcers) in his stomach, he feels he has found the solution to his problem. The solution being another pill, which requires many more dollars, paid to a pharmacy. By this time he is on two medications, one for anxiety and the other for his ulcer disease. The problems have just begun because he may have side effects from the medication.

When his employer finds out that he is on a pill similar to Valium for anxiety, he may tell the person he cannot work around operating machinery. Thus the man may lose his job which adds to his stress. Financial difficulty will now put more stress on his marriage. Added to the financial difficulties and other culminating problems caused by alcohol, his spouse may decide to leave him. She will go to a lawyer and get custody of the children ownership of the house, and this man ends up with the bill. Consequently, this person may have to find another place to live, especially hard now that he does not have a job. He may become homeless. This literally happens every minute and who pays for this? The person who is ill, as well as taxpayers, which includes most of us.

Alcohol also causes liver disease and liver failure. The liver is the organ that detoxifies the toxic byproducts of the body. Now visualize your liver as partially destroyed and you cannot detoxify toxic waste products completely. What will happen? The toxic waste products will start accumulating in your body, affecting your brain and other tissue. When your brain is affected, it is called hepatic encephalopathy. A sign of this disorder is when the person suffering from it literally starts waving "bye-bye" to the world (called asterixis). Hepatic encephalopathy can also cause acute confusional states called delirium, which may be fatal.

So far we have not gone through even 50 percent of the physical damage caused to the body by alcohol.

Alcohol can induce inflammation of the pancreas called pancreatitis, which can be fatal if not treated in a timely manner. Many alcoholics who have been drinking and have chronic gastrointestinal symptoms may not recognize the early symptoms of pancreatitis while intoxicated and they may therefore end up with serious life-threatening illnesses. Alcohol can cause generalized poor nutrition due to the poor eating habits of the alcoholic and poor absorption of various nutrients in the gastrointestinal tract.v Alcohol can also increase the incidence of cancer in the gastrointestinal tract due to the long-term irritant effects of alcohol. Dealing with cancer is certainly not pleasurable, nor is going through any of the painful, uncomfortable treatments associated with it.

Alcohol affects the heart and can cause alcoholic cardiomyopathy, which is irreversible. Alcohol also causes an increase in blood pressure for which many alcoholics may end up taking antihypertensive medications, again after paying hundreds of dollars to their doctors and pharmacists. This could have been avoided simply by stopping drinking and following dietary guidelines, which are described in Chapter 17. Alcohol abuse also causes hardening of the arteries and atherosclerotic cardiovascular diseases.

Once again you are on a pill. Many antihypertensive medications can cause serious side effects such as impotence. When a man is on this drug he can become really worried and develop low self-esteem, thinking his manliness is lost. He can become depressed. In the meantime his spouse is tired of his drinking, his abusive behavior, his not caring for her and the family, and all the negative behavioral patterns that go with the abuse of alcohol. She may file for divorce, take custody of the kids, acquire the house, and send the man out the door. Meanwhile, he may start seeking psychiatric help for depression, anxiety, low self-esteem, and marital problems. In the process, he gets himself another solution to his problems, called an antidepressant such as fluoxetine or some similar drug. (We have solutions for your every problem in healthcare in the form of pills at a cost of hundreds of dollars for an examination and written prescriptions.)

The problem has begun again. As stated above, once you start taking antidepressants, you may have side effects like **impotence.** Now you are really worried again. What is happening to your manliness? **Your wife says something like this: "First you get drunk and do not treat me right. You do not come home on time, you waste our money on booze, you smell bad, you lost your job, you are on all these pills-and the final straw—you can't get it up! Let me find another man! I'm** going to see a lawyer and file for divorce, and by the way I will keep the house, which you have to pay for, and I will ask the lawyer to force you to pay child support, alimony, and the lawyer's bill, which adds up to thousands of dollars, and by then I will be ready for a nice, new man."

Again—who is losing and who is having fun and pleasure, getting rich? Who is having pain—you or the alcohol companies? Ask an alcoholic who has sobered up and he will tell you he has been in this scenario or has seen it being repeated numerous times.

Your lungs and respiratory system are also affected. Many times when people are drinking they have a myth in their minds that alcohol will keep them warm. " I have radiator fluid in me," they think. Thus they will go out in the cold without proper warm clothes on and end up with pneumonia which is caused by a combination of a poor immune system and exposure to cold. This is exacerbated by passing out at night in the cold snow outside of bars. Alcoholics are also prone to developing aspiration pneumonia. This is caused by inhaling vomit, which contains chemicals that cause inflammation and severe damage to their lungs. It can be fatal. **Is this fun?** Pneumonia and bronchitis will also cause decreased oxygenation in the lungs and thus decreased oxygenation throughout your body. It is like your car engine not getting enough fuel to run. What will happen? You are stuttering on every cell level. Is this fun? Again you will need to visit doctors, hospitals and intensive care units all for just a few thousand dollars more. They will give you yet more solutions to your problems—more pills, more tests, more treatments. Remember the old adage: **An ounce of prevention is better than a pound cure.**

And still we are not done. Alcohol affects the nervous system causing damage to the central nervous system as well as the peripheral nervesvi, which is due to the toxic effects of alcohol and malnutrition. It will cause peripheral neuropathy, which causes a loss of sensation in your feet, legs, hands, and penis (causing impotence). Now you have to deal with this issue between your wife and yourself. She thinks you are messing around outside and do not love her. Now you have marital conflict and have to visit marital counselors and sex therapists for few hundred dollars more. You will also have to see a neurologist to be diagnosed and treated. Many times peripheral neuropathy caused by alcohol is almost irreversible. Alcohol abuse is a common cause of male impotence.

On the physical level alcohol can damage the central nervous system, peripheral nervous system, gastrointestinal system, cardiovascular system, respiratory system, and literally every cell in the body, resulting in poor oxygenation, caused by anemia and poor nutrition.

I have been told many times, "But Doctor, I heard drinking a glass of wine is good for your heart." My reply to this is, "It is not alcohol which is good for your heart, but a compound called resveratrol found in grapes and a plant called polygonum." These compounds are powerful antioxidants. Resveratrol lowers the cholesterol and blocks oxidation of low-density lipoproteins, which is a bad type of cholesterol that causes plaque in arteries. Resveratrol also inhibits platelet aggregation and inhibits growth of tumor cells.vii Thus there is no need to drink wine because the protective effects of the resveratrol can be achieved by taking these antioxidants in natural forms or through nutritional supplements without the damaging effects of alcohol.

Alcohol can also cause the emotional and psychological problems of worsening anxiety, depression, nervousness, mood swings, paranoia, hallucinations, impaired judgment, poor concentration, and memory loss.viii People who drink may develop transient paranoia, which is due to several reasons. This paranoia may cause damaging behavior in relationships with others. Many patients I have seen have had alcohol-induced depression and anxiety disorders which required psychiatric

THE TWO MASTERS

medications. Again this will cost visits to the psychiatrist and pharmacist. Employers may hesitate to hire people taking psychiatric medications. (All this can be prevented by not using alcohol). Alcohol seems to be the most frequent cause of teratogenically-induced mental deficiency in the Western world.ix Most psychopharmacological books describe the effects of alcohol on human behavior and judgment. Even as few as two to three servings of alcohol may cause impaired judgment due to its depressant effect on a protective central nervous system, leading to behaviors one would usually not do, such as driving through a red light or stop sign, getting involved with a person in a bar and waking up in the morning in bed with a stranger, which one may regret later, or cursing or abusing a spouse and children. Social implications of this may be disastrous like divorce, catching sexually transmitted diseases, incurring traffic violations, or even vehicular homicide. Alcohol is a common cause in most motor vehicle fatalities and injuries, homicides, and domestic violence in the USA. Imagine what happens to people who are affected by their alcoholic parents. What is their behavior like and who pays the price for this? All of us as taxpayers and insurance subscribers have to bear the burden of increased health care costs and taxes. In 1986 the estimated cost of alcohol abuse in the USA was $128.3 billion. The cost has certainly increased in the last thirteen years. Who is paying this cost? I guess all of us. Accidental death, homicide, and suicide are significant causes of death in the USA. Nearly half of these violent deaths are alcohol-related. During 1987 alcohol-related motor vehicle fatalities numbered 46,386.x Alcohol-related crashes cost society $45 billion, yet the conservative estimate does not include pain, suffering and lost quality of life. These indirect costs raise the alcohol-related crash figure to a staggering $116 billion for 1993. More than 2.6 million drunk driving crashes each year victimize 4 million innocent people who are injured or have their vehicle damaged. Close to 25 percent of people in the USA who carry health insurance have some health care problems that are directly or indirectly related to alcohol. (For more details of economic costs of alcohol abuse refer to Alcohol and Health by the U.S. Department of

Health and Human Services.) Is this fun and pleasurable or is it painful?

Next, alcohol can cause legal problems due to DUI arrests, bar fights, violation of laws, and traffic accidents. Impaired judgment will cause the drinker to take Actions of Disasters for which he or she will have to pay dearly. Is this pleasure or pain? Once you have legal records, they are accessible to most employers. This will lead to difficulty in getting good jobs.

Alcohol has devastating effects on families and children, causing them to have many emotional problems. I had the personal experience of dealing with this numerous times. There is a plethora of information on the psychological ill effects of alcoholic parents on their children. Who pays the price for this? All of us, including people who are directly abused by alcoholics and their children.

Alcohol can cause financial loss and distress due to a multitude of reasons. As mentioned earlier alcohol will cause numerous physical, psychological, emotional, legal, and relationship problems, which will resultantly cost thousands of dollars in doctors' bills, psychiatrists' bills, lawyers' bills, legal fines, and the loss of home, assets, marriage, and employment.

In summary, alcohol causes disastrous effects physically, emotionally, and psychologically in relationships, financially, and ultimately spiritually. Thus, alcohol causes massive amounts of pain in many areas of life. Visualize this in your mind vividly as advertisers create vivid pictures in your mind. Do not reinvent the wheel. Use the same process that advertisers use to link meanings of pleasure to their products except here link pain to that behavior you want to quit.

Most of this information is available in a report produced at taxpayers' expense in the Seventh Special Report to the U.S. Congress in a book Alcohol and Health from the Secretary of Health and Human Services, January 1990.

~~~~~~~~~~~~~~~~~~

THE TWO MASTERS

If I do not drink alcohol I will have pleasure!

Now visualize and feel what will happen and how much pleasure you will have in all areas of life, if you do not drink. If you do not drink how will you feel physically? You will feel better in practically all areas of your body! Visualize the following:

I would not have damaging effects to my brain. I will not have memory loss. I will not incur the toxic effect of alcohol on my brain cells; no head injuries or any bar fights while drunk. I would have better oxygenation to every cell in my body due to no blood loss and therefore no anemia caused by alcohol. This will allow me to function more effectively and improve my job performance and concentration. I would not have the symptoms of depression, anxiety, paranoia and hallucinations caused by alcohol. I will not have to go to psychiatrists, psychologists, or therapists, and pay them hundreds of dollars in fees. I will be saving a bundle of money, which I can use for buying a house, taking vacations, or doing other pleasurable things.

I will feel so much better and my family will be happy to see me sober and spending time with them. I will not have alcohol-induced anxiety, nervousness, depression, or paranoia. I will not be on medications for anxiety or depression (caused by alcohol) and thus I will save a bunch of money. I can avoid side effects from additional medications. I will be winning and having pleasure in many areas of life. I do not have to make alcohol distillers and pharmaceutical companies and related industries rich. I will have the pleasure of saving all that money and utilizing it to benefit my family and myself. I do not have to feel depressed, dysphoric and hung over. I won't feel suicidal and hopeless. I do not have to go to the Emergency Room with suicidal depression while intoxicated. This will certainly help my wife and children respect me.

If I do not drink alcohol, I will not have facial injuries from bar fights, being beaten up by others, and aging due to decreased oxygenation and poor nutrition. I recall that every cell in my body needs oxygen and nutrition. I will look younger and feel better. I will not have a broken nose due to falling down on my face and/or being in bar fights.

Now visualize what will happen to your stomach. If I do not drink, I will not have any irritation in my gastrointestinal tract. I will not have alcohol-induced ulcer disease. I will not have silent bleeding in my gastrointestinal tract and blood loss causing anemia. I will be able to absorb nutrients better in my gastrointestinal tract. Combined with not having anemia, better nutrition, and better eating habits, I will have better oxygenation in my body. Better oxygenation will lead to a better cellular life and greater energy level. I will not be fatigued or tired. I will have better skin, a better appearance, and I will not age as quickly. When I have more energy I can help my family, spend more time with my spouse and children, and do my job properly. When my spouse sees me spending time with her and the family and helping her she will decide to treat me better. This will improve our relationship.

If I do not drink, I do not have to go to the gastroenterologist and have a gastroscopy. This will again save me hundreds of dollars more. I do not have to pay the pharmacy for another drug called ranitidine as I will not have any ulcers. I will not have liver disease and liver failure. I will not have inflammation of the pancreas called pancreatitis. I will have decreased chances of developing gastrointestinal cancers. When I do not drink my heart will function better and my blood pressure will be normal. I will not be on antihypertensive medications, again not paying hundreds of dollars to doctors and pharmacists. This will help me again by creating an abundance of physical energy. I will reduce the chance of hardening of arteries and atherosclerotic cardiovascular diseases.

I will have a reduced chance of developing impotence. This will make my wife happy and help me have better self-esteem. **My wife will say something like this . . . "Honey I love you; you are so nice to me and the kids. I am happy you spend time with us; we have fun together (in bed); and we have more money to do fun things."**

Again who is winning by not drinking and who is losing? Who is having fun and pleasure, getting rich, and who is having pain? You or the alcohol companies? You are the one having pleasure on a long-term basis when you do not drink excessively.

Consider the benefits to the nervous system and the immune system. I will have decreased chances of contracting pneumonia due to the combination of a better immune system and not exposing myself to the cold. Increased oxygenation in my lungs will do my body good and also give me more energy.

If I do not drink I will not have the pain of developing damage to peripheral nerves due to the toxic effects of alcohol and malnutrition. This will decrease the chance of marital conflict. I do not have to visit a neurologist and pay him. I will have the pleasure of saving more money and utilizing it for my family. I will have the pleasure of walking without pain. I will have the pleasure of not becoming impotent and enjoying a sexual relationship. This will help me to build a better relationship with my wife. Quitting alcohol will improve all physical aspects including the central nervous system, peripheral nervous system, gastrointestinal system, cardiovascular system, respiratory system and literally every cell in my body. **I will have the pleasure of having vitality and increased energy.**

Focus next on emotional and psychological health. If I do not drink, I will get rid of anxiety, depression, nervousness, paranoia, hallucinations, impaired judgment, poor concentration, and memory loss caused by alcohol. This will certainly improve my relationships with others. Again this will save the cost of visits to the psychiatrist and pharmacist. I will not have to take psychiatric medications. I will have the pleasure of not having to worry that my employer is going to fire me. My judgment will not be impaired and this will prevent me from taking disastrous actions. This will give me the pleasure of having better social relationships. It will prevent divorce costs, catching sexually transmitted diseases, traffic violations, etc. This will certainly be a benefit to all by saving money wasted in taxpayer dollars and increased insurance premiums. This will save the nation's economy billions of dollars each year.

Think of the relief to yourself in the area of legal problems due to driving under the influence of alcohol or drugs: No more bar fights, violation of laws, or DUI traffic accidents will arise. I will prevent all these by not drinking excess alcohol. This will help the police force to have more time to look into other areas of crime.

Financially there will be rewards. Quitting alcohol will help me financially, as this will prevent the numerous physical, psychological, emotional, legal and relationship problems, which are so costly. It will give me the pleasure of saving emotional energy as well as money and other resources which can be utilized in Actions for Success and Actions for Improvement.

By not drinking alcohol I will have pleasure physically, emotionally and psychologically, in relationships, financially, and ultimately spiritually. Thus I will have massive pleasure by not drinking.

Repeat this intensely, emotionally, and visually in your mind again and again until it becomes a conditioned response. Do this often as television commercials expose you to the repetition of their advertisement messages. Why pay someone on television to link a meaning of pleasure to their product when you can link any beneficial meaning you want in your brain to any idea or concept of your own? Similar techniques can be used to change any destructive, unwanted behavior.

Another Example

A respiratory therapist may still smoke despite knowing emphysema

THE TWO MASTERS

will cause lung disease. Just before she starts smoking she is feeling anxious and nervous due to the perceived stress of her job, or dealing with a family situation, or financial difficulties. So she is feeling pain or discomfort. Her brain has been linked by cigarette commercials to the implication that if she smokes it will help her relax and give her comfort, making her feel she's "come long way, baby" or if she were a man, the link would be that he's really a macho guy.

Basically the act of smoking is still related to her trying to avoid pain and gain some kind of comfort or pleasure. Most people don't think on a long-term basis that smoking will cause ultimate pain. If we master linking pain or pleasure to any event, we can become masters of dealing with even the most difficult problems.

Later in Chapters 6 and 7 we will describe how we can link any meaning to any event. Let us go back to this woman's smoking and what she can do to avoid smoking or to change her habit of smoking. She can use the process or recipe described earlier which helped James to quit smoking. As we have learned earlier, our behavior is always governed by trying to avoid pain and gain some pleasure. If she links a massive amount of pain to continuing smoking and a massive amount of pleasure to quitting smoking and having a healthy life, this will help her to stop smoking. For example, she can start thinking about what will happen to her lungs if she smokes on an ongoing basis. Her lungs, and the oxygenation in her lungs and thus to her oxygen supply in every cell in the body will be adversely affected. If she does not have enough oxygenation to her brain it is going to cause slow gradual deterioration of the brain cells. Imagine this happening for a week, two weeks, three weeks, a month, two months, four months, six months, and then a year, then the next thirty to forty years of her life. *Create a scenario describing how smoking can affect all areas of life over the next year and many more years to come.*

A scenario of how pain and pleasure are linked in a smoker's brain.

Smoking: Avoid pain of boredom/ anxiety/nervousness/stress

Gain pleasure by escaping from boredom/anxiety/nervous feeling

A new scenario of pain and pleasure can be linked which will help the smoker quit.

Visualize how smoking will affect your lungs, causing emphysema, shortness of breath, lung disease, and bad breath. Visualize how smoking will cause a decrease in oxygenation to the brain, heart, liver, kidneys, muscles, and skin, causing damage at a cellular level, causing enhanced aging neuropathy and eventually difficulty in walking long distances or doing any physical tasks. Visualize how emphysema and severe lung disease will cause an inability to participate in the activities of daily living for a week, a month, six months, a year, two years, four years, six years, twenty, forty, and so the numbers go on. Visualize how this will cause pain in most areas of life, thus causing dependence on other people and dependence on various medications and oxygen tanks. Feel the pain and suffering caused by the lung disease which was caused by smoking. Visualize money lost on buying cigarettes and paying doctors' bills.

Then, visualize how, if you stopped smoking, you would have the pleasure of saving money, being able to breathe normally, and have better oxygenation to every cell in the body, thus improving the longevity of all of the different cells in the body, including brain, heart, lungs, liver, kidney, skin, and the nervous system. Imagine how this will improve your life for a week, two weeks, a month, two months, six months, a year, two years, four years, ten years, and forty years.

THE TWO MASTERS

The key here is to link massive pain to continuing smoking and a massive amount of pleasure to living a smoke-free life. If you link enough pain to smoking, your brain will automatically try to take actions to try and stop painful smoking. Most smokers are living with the short-term pleasure of smoking linked into their brain by the cigarette companies.

Another, more immediate way may be go to a hospital or intensive care unit or see pictures of cut sections of a smoker's lung. This is something which will make smokers intensely sick within themselves to the point of feeling nauseous, watching those terribly sick people who are gasping for air. If they have a very intense exposure it will help them to quit smoking, as the intense pain of dreadful diseases will be linked to smoking in their brain. This happened to a secretary who worked with me in the hospital. She had to see her husband dying painfully due to cancer caused by smoking. It was so painful for her to watch her husband dying; it was linked in her brain that cigarette smoking causes a painful death, so she quit smoking.

Let me give you an example of how I demonstrate this in a live seminar. I usually ask people in the audience if they are living in the suburbs and working in the city. If it takes them twenty to twenty five minutes to travel from their workplace in the city to their home, will they be able to reach home in thirty minutes if the traffic is jammed and it is stop and go traffic? Most people in the audience say, "I would not make it home in thirty minutes if the traffic was not moving, especially if it usually takes me twenty to twenty-five minutes when I'm driving at sixty-five to seventy miles per hour. It is impossible." Then I ask them, "If it is absolutely necessary for you to reach home because your son is sick and his life depends on you reaching home in thirty minutes, would you find a way?" Another scenario I give them is, "You will win one million dollars if you reach home in thirty minutes. Now would you reach home in thirty minutes?" Every person of whom I have asked this question answered, "Yes I would, even if I had to drive on the emergency ramp. I would still do it, even if I got a ticket and cops chased me, I would do it." So I asked them, "A few minutes ago you told me this was impossible, and now just two minutes later you say this can be done!" As I say again and again, the ability to find answers is within us. In this scenario I linked a massive amount of pain to not reaching home in thirty minutes and a massive amount of pleasure to reaching home in thirty minutes. This created the necessary force within themselves to find an answer to a problem which they had just considered impossible literally one hundred twenty seconds earlier.

The ability to create anything and the ability to deal with any challenge is within all of us. If you master pain and pleasure, you can tap into this inner resource that all of us have.

> *The mind is its own place, and in itself can make heaven of hell and hell of heaven.*
> Milton

---

[i] A.C Bhaktivedanta Swami Prabhupada. Bhagavad-Gita As It Is. 6th Printing. Los Angeles: Bhaktivedanta Book Trust, 1994.

[ii] Illinois Transportation Department. National Highway and Traffic Safety Board,

[iii] Harold I. Kaplan, M.D. and Benjamin J. Saddock, M.D. Synopsis of Psychiatry, Behavioral Sciences Clinical Psychiatry. Maryland: Williams & Wilkins, 1988.

[iv] U.S. Dept. of Health and Human Services. Alcohol and Health. January 1990, National Institute on Alcohol Abuse and Alcoholism.

[v] See note iii above.

[vi] Louis S. Goodman and Alfred Gilman. Goodman and Gilman's, The Pharmacologic Basis of Therapeutics. New York: Macmillan Publishing Co., Inc., 1980.

[vii] Glen A. Halvorson M.D. Stop Burning Hole in Your Brain, Revolutionary Nutrient Restores and Protects Your Health. Topanga, Calif.: Lumenhealth Enterprises, 1997. (Research had been done by the University of Illinois.)

[viii] See note iii above.

[ix] See note vi above.

Chapter 5

Action vs. Inaction

One difference between successful people and people who do not succeed is the habit of consistent, daily actions. Many people possess plenty of knowledge, education, and ability, but they fail to take action. Take this example of coming up with an idea for creating a new product, method, or some service and marketing it to become wealthy: Did you ever have an idea which you felt was marketable but for which you failed to take actions to reach your goal? Later on you found out that somebody else came up with a similar idea, manufactured it, mass marketed it, and became successful. The difference between the person who is actually marketing the product and the person who just has the idea is that the first person consistently takes action.

Another example I see in the hospital all the time are the health care professionals with extensive knowledge that they should keep their weight in control, should not smoke or drink excessively, and should not abuse narcotics, yet they fail to live healthy lifestyles. So many health care professionals are overweight, smoke, abuse drugs and alcohol, and have preventable health problems despite all the knowledge they possess. They know they should be eating healthy food and exercising regularly. However, they have failed to use their knowledge to follow through or take actions. The difference between them and people who are healthy is that the people who are healthy take actions consistently to stay fit.

A huge factor in being successful is to take action. Knowledge is not enough to be successful. One must follow through by taking daily actions on an ongoing basis while using knowledge to reach goals. I have a friend who has two bachelor degrees (one in nursing and one in chemistry), and in addition he has learned literally hundreds of trades, from working on cars to building a house to being a salesmen, and many more. When you ask him any questions about anything in these areas, he has so much knowledge he can advise you for hours. However, he has never gotten any results for himself, because he has never followed through by taking consistent daily action.

Knowledge is not enough. Knowledge combined with daily consistent actions will create results.

Let us look into what causes people to procrastinate and stops them from taking action. As we studied in the chapter on "The Two Masters," our brain is constantly trying to avoid pain and seeking what is pleasurable. So when someone is procrastinating and putting off taking action, they have linked pain to taking actions and pleasure to not taking actions or procrastinating. Unless we master linking pleasure to taking action and pain to procrastinating, or not taking action, we will continue the pattern of not taking action. What usually happens when we procrastinate, or put off taking action, is that we say to ourselves, "Let me just watch TV . . . read . . . tan . . . or do some other restful activity," as we have linked pain to taking action. By using the techniques described in Chapters 4 and 6, we can link the meaning of pleasure to taking action and the meaning of pain to procrastination.

Write down your goals. Write down the actions that you need to take to reach your goals. Write down why you do not take action. Then write down in detail what would happen if you do not take action to reach these goals and how it will create pain. Then write down what pleasure you will feel reaping the benefits you will get if you take action to reach the goals. In summary, write down the old pain-pleasure pattern, which was driving you to procrastinate and then create a new pain-pleasure pattern, which will drive you to take some action. Start

ACTION VS. INACTION

taking those actions now and every day consistently. As you take actions, check the course of your actions to ensure you are going toward your goals. If you are going away from your goals, change the course of actions in order to be directed toward the goals.

> *"One definition of insanity is to keep doing the same things and expect different results."* (Author unknown)

As you progress toward a goal, your brain will be more enthused to see the results and this will promote taking more actions. It is important to condition our mind to take action and have pleasure associated with the results. Reward yourself even when you have a small, positive result every step of the way toward your goal. Remember how they train dolphins in Sea World by rewarding them. Positive conditioning will give better results, as our brain is always looking for pleasure. As we said earlier keep your goal in sight all the time to hit the bull's-eye.

Remember every action or inaction will create a result. Decide which results you want, and choose the action which will empower you and propel you towards your goals.

Check for your disempowering beliefs, e.g., "I decide my potential based upon what others perceive as possible or impossible, which limits me in trying to broaden my horizons and fulfilling a bigger potential." Another disempowering act is to tell yourself something is impossible. Unless you change your disempowering belief systems, you will have tremendous difficulty taking action and achieving your goal. We need to realize that we are the ones who limit ourselves, and we are the only ones who stop ourselves from trying bigger goals. For example, we often say to ourselves, "I am afraid of failure."

When I asked some Vietnam War veterans to write down their disempowering belief system, their answers were revealing as follows:

1. Getting close to someone will cause pain. (This is often due to close friends dying in Vietnam.)
2. Do not trust anyone; especially do not trust authority figures as they will betray you. (This is due to the way authority figures treated them in combat or after returning from Vietnam.)
3. Rain will bring pain, danger or sadness. (Friends died while it was raining or they were attacked by the Vietcong during rain.)
4. Do not sit with your back to the door; the enemy could attack you. You have to know where the enemy is coming from at all times.

These disempowering beliefs have caused many Vietnam veterans difficulty in taking actions towards their goals. They have trouble maintaining relationships, resulting in multiple marriages and difficulty getting close to anyone; they cannot trust their bosses, get angry easily and lose jobs; they feel sad or depressed when it starts to rain; and they are often unable to go to restaurants or the mall without being hyper-vigilant.

Another example is a woman I treated with a disempowering belief that marriage is losing freedom; marriage means losing identity and losing the pleasure of the attention of many men. This was linked in her brain during earlier years of her life. Could she take actions to stay in her marriage with these disempowering beliefs? Guess what would happen to her marriage. Unless one has an empowering belief that marriage is a union, and being bonded to each other creates pleasure in two people sharing life, it will be a disaster.

Here is another quick way to see if you are taking actions to reach your goals: Make a list of all the activities you do in a day including sleep, watching TV, spending time with friends, time spent on meals, movies, and all other activities. Then check how many hours you spent in each activity. Then check how many hours you have spent on activities which will take you toward your goal. For example if your goal is to create financial freedom, but you spend ten hours in sleep,

ACTION VS. INACTION

four to five hours in watching TV and two to three hours in a bar, you will soon find that you have spent less than one hour in activities related to achieving your goals. In this case you are certainly not taking daily consistent actions towards your goal.

Remember we all have same twenty-four hours of time in a day and basically most of us have similar equipment: two hands, two legs, and a head with average to above-average intelligence. The people who became millionaires or produced world-changing results have the same twenty-four hours a day. What makes a difference is what they do with that time. Look at the following charts. The chart on the left gives an example of how a successful person may spend twenty-four hours of time. The chart on the right indicates how another person may waste the same amount of time.

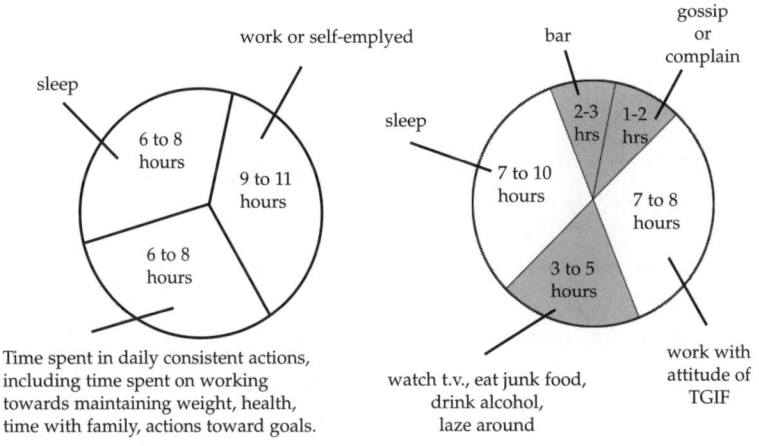

Everyone has twenty-four hours a day!

Time spent in daily consistent actions, including time spent on working towards maintaining weight, health, time with family, actions toward goals.

watch t.v., eat junk food, drink alcohol, laze around

Grey area indicates time wasted each day out of 24 hours. Multiply that by 365 days a year!

The basic difference between people who are successful and not so successful is what successful people do in their twenty-four hours each day by taking consistent actions focusing on their goals. They do not waste time. Consistent daily goal directed actions produce results and success. Knowledge without actions will not produce results. To be successful one must make use of knowledge you gain from this or any other self-help book. To quote Herbert Spencer, "The great aim of education is not knowledge but action."

We learned in this chapter:

1. Consistent daily actions will produce results.
2. Link massive pain to not taking actions and ultimate pain to inaction.
3. Make a list of disempowering beliefs, and get rid of disempowering beliefs.
4. Make a list of empowering beliefs, and strengthen empowering beliefs. (Chapter 15 will give you exercises on how to select an empowering belief system.)
5. As you take daily actions, check your course of actions to see that you are progressing toward your goal.
6. Reward yourself for the slightest positive results from the actions toward your goal.

One who restrains the senses of actions but whose mind dwells on sense objects certainly deludes himself and is called a pretender (hypocrite). Perform your prescribed duty, for doing so is better than not working. One cannot maintain one's body without work.

(Bhagavad-Gita)

---

[i] A.C Bhaktivedanta Swami Prabhupada. Bhagavad-Gita As It Is. Los Angeles: Bhaktivedanta Book Trust, 1994

Chapter 6

Conditioned Responses

I once wondered why Vietnam veterans would jump when the doors were slammed. I was running post-traumatic stress disorder program, and I observed that whenever a door slammed the Vietnam vets would jump or get startled. Similarly when a car backfired the veterans would jump or get startled. "Why do you jump?" I posed. Many replied that the door slam reminded them of gunfire. They felt scared, fearful, or a sense of danger. But why would they react that way even when they were sitting in a safe place in the state of Missouri with no war going on?

I studied other stimuli that made these people jump or startle. I researched when this had happened for the first time. The first time this occurred was approximately twenty-five to thirty years ago when they were in the war in combat. With gunfire around them, they felt fearful, frightened, hyper-alert, or a combination of these feelings. **The stimulus (trigger) of the sound of gunfire and the intense state of mind** became linked in the veteran's brain. By this time, most Vietnam War veterans and their therapists have recognized door slams, cars backfiring, and the Fourth of July, as triggers for Vietnam War veterans.

"Intense state of mind" and "triggers" are two essential components of conditioned responses in this scenario. Whenever we are in an intense state of mind if there is any physical trigger going on, the intense state of mind and the trigger get linked together in the brain. In other words, the brain links fearfulness to door slamming, or fear of death to a helicopter sound. This is no different than Ivan Pavlov and his dog. What did Pavlov do? He would bring food to the dog, which would put the dog in an intense state of hunger, and then he would ring the bell. He repeated this scenario many times. Eventually he stopped bringing the food and would just ring the bell. He noticed the dog would start salivating due to the recreation of an intense state of hunger. The following examples will give you an idea how these two components are linked together in Vietnam War veterans.

Triggers	Senses	States of Mind
Door slam	**Hearing**	fearful
Car backfire	**Hearing**	hyper-alert
Fireworks	**Hearing**	frightened
Helicopter sound	**Hearing**	fear of death life saving
Tree line	**Sight**	life in danger
Certain terrain	**Sight**	sense of danger
VA hospital	**Sight**	anger
US government	**Sight**	betrayal/ no trust
Friend	**Sight**	pain of death/loss
Wife touching them	**Touch**	hyper-alert/ attack mode
Certain food	**Taste**	feeling enemy has poisoned food
Jet fuel/diesel fuel	**Smell**	hyper-alert/ fearful

The triggers can be sound, sight, smell, touch, taste-any of the five senses.

We are exposed to different events all the time. For a woman who is raped in an elevator, the elevator becomes linked as a trigger to the intense state of mind, of being frightened, feeling disgusted, degraded,

CONDITIONED RESPONSES

depressed, and hopeless. Advertisers do this to us all the time, except in advertising you need many repetitions for these two things to be linked. For example, an experience of being raped will link a feeling of fear to the elevator via an intense state of mind whereas, "I need brand name shoes to feel good," requires many repetitions to link having the shoes to feeling good.

Let us examine how a conditioned response is formed. We will have to go back twenty-five or thirty years ago to see what happened in the Vietnam War. The following three diagrams explain, first, how feelings of fear or hyper-alertness were linked to gunfire (**sound**); second, how feelings of sadness or depression or friends dying was linked to rain; and third, how hunger or food is linked to the ringing of the bell.

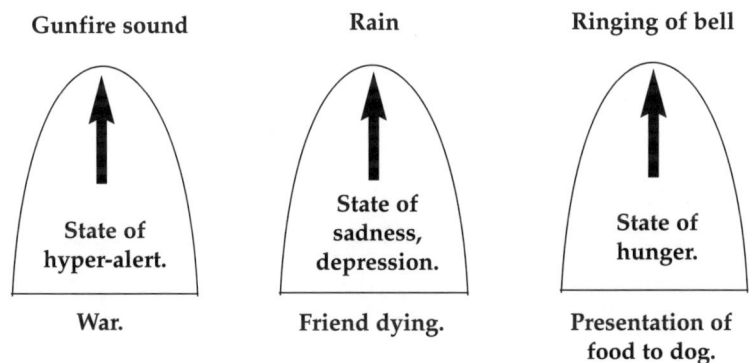

Let us compare two different conditioned responses to the same triggers or stimuli in two brothers. John and Roger were twin brothers raised on a farm in Kansas. They grew up helping their father farm. When John was eighteen years old, he was drafted into the U.S. Army. After his basic training and advanced infantry training at Fort Leonardwood, he was sent to Vietnam. While on his tour of duty in Vietnam he observed a lot of horrifying scenarios including his friends being killed. Whenever it was raining in Vietnam, Vietcong enemies attacked them and John's closest friend was killed during one of those attacks.

On the other hand, Roger met a South American woman when he was eighteen years old. He was dating her and she told him they should go to South America to have some fun. She was a gorgeous woman and Roger found that whenever it was raining in South America, they had fabulous sex. The woman told him that the rainy season is the time to be romantic in Latin culture. Roger had a ball visiting South America and had a wonderful romantic time.

After a year both John and Roger returned home to the United States to their father's farm. John came back from Vietnam and Roger returned from his romantic escapade in South America. Their father told them it was time to go back to work, and one day when they were both busy on the farm, it started raining. As it began to rain John began to feel depressed and sad, but didn't know why. On the other hand, Roger walked up to John and said, "John I must find a woman and get romantic!" John told him, "You're crazy! I'm feeling sad and depressed with the rain, and you're aroused!"

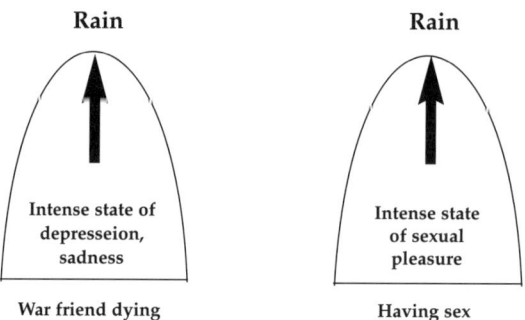

Why would these two brothers have two different responses to rain? One gets depressed and saddened, and the other one becomes sexually excited. It basically relates to their two different intense states of mind during rain. Thus, rain was linked to two entirely different meanings in their individual brains. The above diagrams illustrate how this happens.

CONDITIONED RESPONSES

The above phenomenon explains how meanings get linked in the brain all the time. After this link is established we begin to think the phenomenon is real. For example, when we are little babies we have no concept that touching fire will cause us pain. Our parents try to teach us not to touch the fire, because we will get burned. How did we discover that? Someday, accidentally, we touch a flame of fire, which puts us in an intense, painful state of mind. What was the trigger at that time? The flame of fire. Thus, the intense state of mind and trigger became linked in our brain. The book Neuro-Linguistic Programming uses the term "anchor"i instead of "trigger." This book presents numerous examples of how different meanings become linked in the brain. Advertisers do this to us all the time. They teach us that we need a soft drink for pure refreshment and require a credit card to feel secure and have fun on vacation.

Here are some of my own experiences of how different states of mind became linked to different triggers unknowingly to me. Early one morning I left with my children in a new van driving through rural areas of Alabama on a divided highway bound for Florida. The tall pine trees on both sides of the road were almost touching each other at the top of the road. Beyond the pine trees we could see a small valley filled with a fine, misty fog. The sun was just rising and I felt intensely peaceful driving on that rural highway early in the morning. I was so touched by this feeling that I asked my daughter to take a photograph of the road. We were listening to music given to me by my spiritual teacher and the feelings of intense peace lasted for about three or four hours while driving.

A couple of years later I was driving through some of the roughest neighborhoods in Kansas City, with heavy traffic due to road and street repairs being done. Usually while driving in those areas I would feel anxious or hyper-alert because of the high crime in that area, but I was playing the same cassette tape mentioned above, which I had listened to on the way to Florida, and it brought back intense feelings of peace, joy, and bliss. Upon reaching the Veterans' Affairs Hospital to conduct classes, I shared this experience with some of the Vietnam War veterans.

Why would I feel intense peace, joy, and bliss while driving through busy, rough neighborhoods? Unknowingly, the music I had been listening to on the way to Florida was linked to the intense feelings of peace, blissfulness, and joy which I had experienced during that morning drive through Alabama. Having discovered that this particular music could put me in an intense state of peace, joy, and blissfulness, I began using that tape to bring on peace and joy instantly whenever driving in city traffic.

Another example of this phenomenon occurs when I listen to music performed by the group Enigma. This music makes me feel intensely energetic and powerful. I had to run two miles in eighteen-and-a-half minutes for my Army reserves physical fitness test and I was practicing the two-mile runs with my children encouraging and cheering me on. I could barely finish the run in eighteen minutes, but decided to experiment with the phenomenon of a trigger attached to certain state of mind to try to improve my speed. At the beginning of the run for the physical fitness test I put on headphones and started listening to the music of Enigma. To my shock I finished the two-mile run in fifteen-and-a-half minutes! I had never run that fast in my life. How did I manage to achieve those results? My body had not changed from the previous day of practicing with the children. What changed was my state of mind and this created phenomenal results in me. In this case, the music (trigger) was linked to the intense state of feeling powerful and energetic.

The intense state of mind can be positive (empowering) or negative (disempowering). Following are some examples of empowering and disempowering states of mind.

CONDITIONED RESPONSES

Positive States of Mind	Negative States of Mind
(Empowering)	(Disempowering)
Joy/happiness	Depression
Peace/blissfulness	Anger/hostility
Invincibility	Fear/panic/anxiety
Powerful	Frightened/hyper-alert
Energetic/enthusiastic	Betrayal/cannot trust
Compassion	Guilt
Fulfillment	Hopelessness/helplessness
Salesmanship	Sense of no future

We can link either positive or negative states of mind to any triggers. Most of the time these different states of mind are linked unknowingly in our brain by someone else. Various states of mind can be linked to different triggers/anchors, as happened with the Vietnam War veterans. The following are examples of links in Vietnam War veterans:

Rain

State of depresseion, sadness.

War friend dying.

Diesel fuel

State of fear, hyper-alert.

Attack by enemy with armored vehicle.

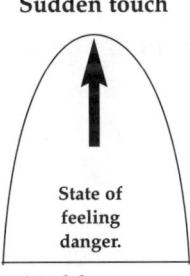

Sudden touch

State of feeling danger.

Attack by enemy in tunnel.

We can use this phenomenon on different triggers. The triggers can be any of your five senses: touch, taste, smell, sound, and sight. However, we need to choose a trigger, which we can carry with ourselves all the time. For example, if you wish to feel powerful and romantic when asking for a date, you can link a powerful state to listening to music but to create this romantic and powerful state when approaching a woman, you would have to carry a boom box. Linking this state to music may not be practical. You want to choose a trigger, easily accessible to the person using it and inconspicuous to others, which basically means choosing some type of unique, personalized signal or touch. You can choose different types of unique touches or different words, said aloud with intensity, for different states of mind. For example:

Touch 1: Touch left forefinger: Feeling peaceful.
Touch 2: Make a fist: Feeling invincible/powerful.
Touch 3: Touch your chin: Feeling energetic.

Let me give an illustration of a Vietnam War veteran and what he did. This veteran was always extremely angry, irritable and cursed people. I asked him during our seminar, "Do you ever feel peaceful?" Initially, the veteran replied "no." But after thinking for a few minutes he said, "Yes, when I get up early in the morning and sit by myself in the family room watching the aquarium and seeing the fish swim from one end to the other, I feel very peaceful. My wife is still sleeping." That veteran had a recipe for peace, he just did not know it! I suggested he utilize the recipe to feel peaceful by following the exact ingredients, portions, and steps. The ingredients in this case include the early morning, his family room, and the aquarium with swimming fish. The portions include him being alone without his wife, and the steps are sitting in front of the aquarium early in the morning, by himself. As long as he followed the same recipe, he would have the same results of creating peacefulness.

I asked him to link that state of peacefulness to a trigger. The veteran chose to rub his right forefingers together while in the family room in a peaceful state of mind. As long as he practices this for two to three weeks, the intense state of peacefulness and the trigger will become linked in his brain. After a few weeks, all he needs to do is to rub his fingers, even if he is in another situation, and that will bring him peace. This is no different than the door slamming which caused the veterans

CONDITIONED RESPONSES

to be frightened or hyper-alert. Another example of this is Pavlov's dog. The bell rings and the dog begins to salivate. The following diagrams will make this clear.

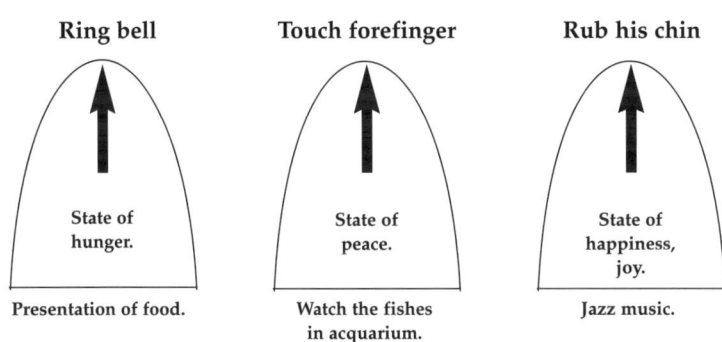

Let me illustrate another example. My friend Perry wanted to know how he could feel joyous whenever he wished to. I asked Perry the same question, "Do you ever feel joyous?" and he replied, "Yes, when I listen to jazz music and I am alone." I explained to him how he had his own recipe for feeling joyous. He should follow the same recipe with the same ingredients, portions, and steps. "While you are in a joyous state, at the peak state of this joyousness, you should link it to a touch of some particular quality." Perry chose to touch his chin with his left hand while feeling joyous, listening to jazz. After many repetitions he realized that he felt joyous whenever he touched his chin, even when he was not listening to jazz. This should clarify how triggers or anchors get attached to an intense state of mind. Neuro-linguistic programming as demonstrated by Charles Faulkner in Neuro-Linguistic Programming[ii] and Anthony Robbins in Unlimited Power[iii] gives various techniques of anchoring positive, empowering states of mind.

Let us study in detail how these states of mind are linked to triggers in the brain. Most of the time this happens unknowingly throughout our lives. Commercials use similar techniques to condition our mind. Let us compare a commercial and the frightening experience of being raped.

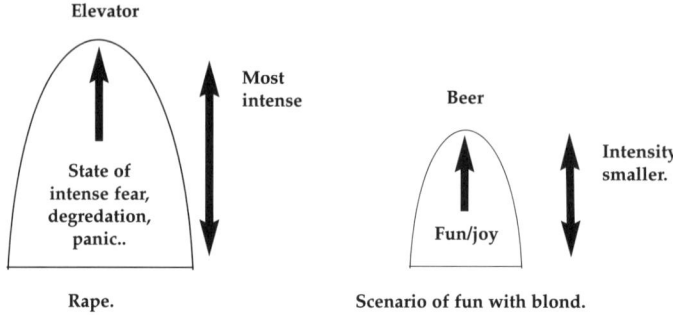

Experience of being raped in the elevator

TV Commercial for beer

The experience of being raped is a catastrophically intense experience, which occurred in an elevator. Thus, the elevator (trigger) is linked to intense feelings of fear, anger, humiliation, degradation, depression, and panic with one exposure. On the other hand, feeling good or having fun is linked to drinking a beer and needs repeated exposure to get linked. The less intense the experience, the more repetition it needs to get linked in the brain. Another example of this is an experience of a friend being killed in war while the sounds of gunfire are going off all around. Thus, the sound of gunfire may be linked in the Vietnam War veteran's brain to the fearful feelings of death and dying after just one or two exposures.

Once the trigger and intense state of mind are linked together, the brain is on auto-pilot. Most of our behavior and thinking processes are a result of conditioned responses. This book provides examples of numerous conditioned responses within us. Most of us are a by-product of millions of conditioned responses repeated throughout our lives.

For example, I asked one of the veterans in a seminar, "If you're raised in a redneck town in the southwest area of Missouri how would

CONDITIONED RESPONSES

you perceive a foreigner or person of another race?" The veteran replied honestly "I would think that as a foreigner, you are out to get my job." I asked another one "If you're raised in the ghetto with all poor people, how would you perceive people who are wealthy?" He replied, "Rich people are snobs, and I would think of using a means of violence to get even with them." Then I asked him, "If you were raised from birth in China what language would you be speaking and what culture would you follow?" The veteran replied "Chinese, because my mind would be conditioned for the Chinese lifestyle and ways of thinking."

Let us examine a trigger like rain on a cloudy day and how it is linked in different people's minds. For example, a Vietnam War veteran thinks about death, dying, sadness, and fear when exposed to rain. What about people who have not been in a war but observe weather forecasts on television each day? They feel a rainy day is a crummy day. Let us examine how that happens.

Vietnam veteran whose friend was killed on a rainy day.

Weather forecast viewer who hears frequently that the rainy day is a crummy day. He begins to believe all rainy days are crummy days.

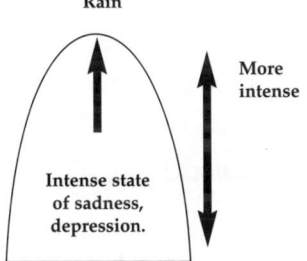

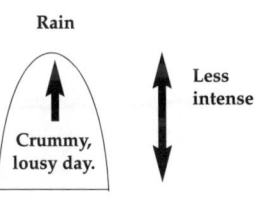

When I came to USA from India and began watching the weather forecast I wondered why they called a rainy day a "crummy, lousy day"

but a sunny day was a "beautiful day." When I began studying the people who live longer in different parts of the world I realized that many of them did not have the same concept that rainy days are crummy days. Whether it was raining or sunny or snowing, they went about their business without the weather affecting their emotional state. In fact, looking back on my own life, I realized that when it was raining or the sun was shining I went on doing my own daily activities without feeling lousy. We will discuss in other chapters how different conditioned responses affect our emotional states, our behavior, our psychoneuroimmunological status and then affect us physically. We will discuss in detail how advertisers purposely link and create different responses. Commercials use conditioned responses to sell products and make a buck.

I want to emphasize that we attach different meanings to events and objects around us. Most of the time these meanings attach unknowingly to different triggers, and based upon this attached meaning, we live out our lives. Some of these meanings can be empowering to us but others can also be disempowering to us. For example, two friends go to the oceanfront and look at the high waves. One friend becomes panicked, frightened, anxious and wants to get away from there. When he gets frightened and anxious, his heart starts beating faster, his blood pressure may go up, he may feel uncomfortable in the stomach and may feel nervous all over his body. When he perceives fear and stress, his body triggers complex biological mechanisms secreting adrenaline, noradrenaline, cortisol, and other chemical messengers which are harmful psychoneuroimmunologically to his body.[iv] This basically creates disempowering feelings and changes his body's physiology.

On the other hand, his friend who enjoys surfing, gets excited looking at the waves crashing. He wants to take his surfboard into the water and go surfing. This friend feels happy, excited, and elated when he's looking at the crashing waves. When he feels that way he has a joyous feeling, not only in his head, but also all over his body and actually changes his body physiology. His body secretes interferon and interleukin, which are beneficial to his body.[v]

How does it happen that two friends looking at the same event have totally different emotional and physical reactions? It is because each has attached a different meaning to the same event. One has attached the meaning of fear, panic, and danger to the high waves, but the other friend has attached the meaning of joy, excitement, and pleasure to them. Thus, it is important for us to know how we attach meaning to different events or objects and it would be useful and beneficial for all of us to link meanings which are empowering to us, as well as beneficial to all.

Let's take the example of the **"Thank God It's Friday"** syndrome. What do the people think who believe in TGIF? They look forward to the weekend. What do they want to do on weekends? They want to have fun and party. The meaning of having fun and partying being attached to the weekend has been instilled into their heads by someone who wants to make a buck. What do those people do on the weekend anyway? They may get drunk, do drugs, may go to nightclubs or do something on the weekend that they may not even remember on Monday mornings. Imagine if they are our employees and have to come to work on Monday mornings for us. What is their state of mind on Monday morning? "What the heck am I doing at work on Monday morning?" "Work sucks!"

In seminars I asked the audience, "When people come to work with this attitude, are they able to focus on their work, concentrate on their work, and put energy into getting their work done?" Most audience members answer this question "No, they're not interested in doing their work on Monday morning, and are not focused on their work. They are focused on the next weekend coming up." Now what's going to happen? They also have a calendar sitting on the desk with Wednesday marked as **hump day**. Basically, they are not interested in putting their efforts into their jobs. If you are their boss, and if you see these people are not doing their work, what would you do? You would probably chew them out. Then these people would jump up and say, "Now work really sucks!" When they feel work sucks and live with the TGIF syndrome it's not only happening in their heads, it's happening all over their bodies. In the next chapter, we'll explain, in detail, how these disempowering attitudes affect our body physiology and immune system.

Where did these people get this meaning of TGIF in their head? Apparently it was linked into their brain by either an advertiser wanting to make a buck who does not care how it affects the rest of society, or a well-meaning but misguided relative who also believed in TGIF. Think about the people who get drunk and have parties, how it affects their own health and then their families, and their employers. If you calculate the physical, emotional, legal, and work related costs related to the TGIF syndrome it would amount to billions of dollars. Who is paying this cost? All of us, because when people get intoxicated or abuse drugs and have accidents everyone else's insurance premiums go up. When they go to doctors everyone else's premiums rise. When they get arrested, the taxpayers pay for their stay in prison. Anyone who goes to prison in the United States costs the taxpayers approximately $40,000 per year. Who pays these costs? All of us. If someone commits homicide while intoxicated and goes to prison for ten years, it will cost taxpayers nearly half a million dollars!

If we master what meaning we want to attach to any event and make sure that meaning is empowering to all, it will be a win-win situation. Chapter 3, **Actions for Success**, provided details on how to screen any actions to be successful.

If you look at many commercials, you will realize that destructive meanings may be linked to products purely for profit motives. Cigarette

CONDITIONED RESPONSES

smoking is a prime example. Ask any smoker about his reaction when he first started smoking. Most smokers will tell you they started coughing and choking, and did not like the taste of the tobacco. They did not like the sensations that went along with the first puff of the cigarette. So why did they continue to smoke? Because the people who sell tobacco linked into their brain, "You will be cool if you smoke." "You've come a long way, Baby." "You will be a macho man riding a horse if you have a cigarette in your hand or mouth." "If you smoke a cigar you are an important, prestigious person." Here is an example of an unpleasant experience from the first puff of smoke but still they can successfully attach a meaning of pleasure to it. Does it work; did it work? It works on millions of people everyday, all over the world, because millions smoke despite knowing it can cause cancer, emphysema, heart disease, neuropathies, and death. Do you see how we can link a meaning of pleasure to even a disgusting practice such as smoking?

Let us take the next example. You have seen the beer commercials where they show you have to drink their beer to enjoy a football game. All the scientific studies done by neuropsychologists clearly indicate that even having a few drinks will impair your ability to perceive events clearly around you, for example, driving or doing complex tasks which involve using all of your five senses. Alcohol costs the United States close to $200 billion per year. Approximately 25 percent of Americans who have private health insurance have medical or psychological problems that may be related to alcohol in one way or another. *(If you are interested in more statistics on alcohol-related costs, contact a local Alcoholics Anonymous or Mothers Against Drunk Driving chapter.)*

Alcohol affects your brain, your gastrointestinal tract, your respiratory system, your cardiovascular system, and your neurological system, as well as having devastating effects on you legally, financially, and emotionally. Who pays this cost? All of us, through increased medical bills, increased funding for more prisons, increased insurance premiums, and increased taxes. Our families must face the devastating effects of alcohol in literally all areas of our lives, directly or indirectly.

Take this example: If I live in a nice neighborhood with literally no crime, I feel I am safe in my home with an alarm system that is installed and activated. Why should I worry about someone getting drunk downtown and beating up his wife? I may think I am sitting safely in my home; I don't have to worry about this man. However, I need to understand that when this man gets drunk, beats up his wife, and is charged with family violence by the state, his legal costs are going to be paid by the taxpayers. His wife goes to a state mental health clinic because she has no private insurance and we as taxpayers have to pay for the costs incurred. When this man gets a DUI and is arrested we must pay for that with our taxpayer money and if he kills someone while drunk that person has paid with his life.

Why did this man start drinking in the first place? Because someone put a meaning in his head that drinking is "cool," drinking is going to make him a "macho man," drinking will make him "enjoy life." In fact, alcohol companies studied how they can get more people to drink. People always want to be somebody and want to have some significance in their life. The advertiser portrays that if you want to be a successful lawyer you should be having martinis at lunch. If you want to be a sharp-shooting cowboy, you have got to have a beer. If you are a young man and want to have fun, you need to have a beer. If you are a woman and want to be fashionable and chic, drink our champagne. If you are a family man and you want to enjoy a holiday meal, you have got to have wine. If you want to be a successful politician, you must have cocktails. Basically, what alcohol companies have done is to link either pleasure or significance to consuming their product.

CONDITIONED RESPONSES

There are two components I want to suggest here: First, how we link a pleasurable meaning to a destructive event; second, how advertisers in their commercials link meanings to their products without caring how destructive it may be to all of us eventually. If all of us, collectively, would look at how we can give empowering meanings to any event (meanings that will be beneficial to ourselves as well as our fellow human beings), it will be a win-win situation.

Here is another harsher example of how a meaning of pleasure was linked to a most horrifying event. Do you remember the event in California when a group of people committed mass suicide after castrating themselves waiting for aliens? Why would they do such a horrible thing? Because someone successfully managed to link a meaning of pleasure to castrating themselves and the anticipation of going to heaven or another planet.

This is no different than the Japanese teaching their young men to be kamikaze suicide bombers. All they had to do was to tell the young men that they would have the ultimate pleasure in life, and they and their families would be honored in the history of Japan if they would kill themselves while killing the enemy by the suicide bombing of Allied ships. Most of the Arab countries link similar meaning in their young children's minds to the effect that they will go to heaven if they kill their enemies. This is known as act of Jihad. Look at how an event as ultimately destructive as killing yourself is linked to being pleasurable or bringing a sense of honor.

These examples illustrate how even horrifying events can be linked to feelings of pleasure by repeated conditioning. If we can all learn to link empowering meanings to any event, a meaning which will be beneficial to the self as well as to the rest of the human race, it will be a win-win situation for all.

A larger conditioned response will override a smaller one.

Remember how the Vietnam War veterans mastered how to feel joyous and relaxed after practicing the previous techniques? He listened to jazz, which made him feel joyous and relaxed and then linked that to touching his chin with his left hand. He commented later, "Doc, I can get relaxed by touching my chin with my left hand, but when my

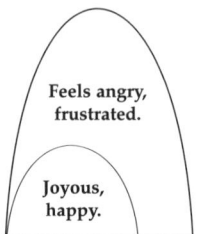

Wife nagging and starting fight.

wife walks in and starts nagging me, it doesn't work. I get frustrated and angry. This technique you've been teaching doesn't work for me." In this case we need to learn how to override a negative conditioned response. The answer to this is within itself. For example, in this veteran's case why would his wife's nagging make him frustrated? The above diagram will explain why this happens.

If you look at the diagrams it is apparent why a negative response overrides a positive response. It is due to the fact that the negative response is much bigger than the positive response. The negative responses are stacked on each other due to repeated conflicts with the wife over a period of time, thus creating larger negative conditioned responses. In this case seeing the wife complaining can be a trigger that will fire off the negative responses of anger, frustration, etc. Thus, the solution to undo any conditioned response lies in the above example itself. Any bigger response, or massive response, will override a smaller conditioned response. If you create a massive, positive, conditioned response it will override the literally smaller, negative response.

CONDITIONED RESPONSES

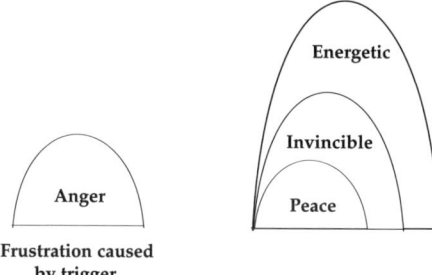

Frustration caused by trigger.

This is demonstrated by the above diagram.

This needs practice and repetition in order to be implemented successfully, just as when you were learning to drive a car. When you first learned to drive you looked at the accelerator pedal and your mind was on the pedal, not the road. When you shifted gears using a manual transmission there were difficulties coordinating your movements at first. When you were learning to change lanes and looked into the side view mirror, you unknowingly pulled the car into the lane on the side where you looked. However, after months of practice you drove effortlessly without trying to coordinate these movements and yet still were able to look for appropriate street signs and billboards, or listen to music, etc. Eventually you learned to do these things automatically, a positive conditioned response.

Thus, in the above veteran's case we taught him to link many positive conditioned responses to one trigger. This can be done in a two-step process. The first step is to link different positive states of mind to different triggers/anchors. The second step is to link all of those to one trigger. The following diagram illustrates this.

Positive States of Mind	**Triggers**
Feeling joyous/happy	Rubbing uniquely the forefinger
Feeling invincible/powerful	Rubbing uniquely middle finger
Feeling energetic	Rubbing uniquely ring finger

Once you master having these three or four different positive states of mind on these three or four fingers or three or four different triggers, by rubbing all three of these fingers simultaneously you have a much bigger positive response. One can also link multiple positive conditioned responses to one trigger. Unique words or sounds can also be used as triggers. Another thing you can do is increase the intensity of positive responses. This is just one technique to override a negative emotional response. Most of these techniques are based upon how the brain erases other past conditioned responses unknowingly. More detailed descriptions of these techniques can be found in Neuro-Linguistic Programming The New technology of Achievement by Charles Faulkner or Unlimited Power by Anthony Robbins.

Remember the most intense response will override the less intense response.

What would you attempt to do if you knew you could not fail?
(Dr. Robert Schuller)

---

[i] Robert Dilts, John Grinder, Richard Bandler, Leslie Bandler, Judith DeLozier. Neuro-Linguistic Programming: The Study of the Structure of Excellence. Cupertino, CA: Meta Publications, 1980.
[ii] Charles Faulkner, Gerry Schmidt, Robert McDonald, Tim Hallbom, Suzi Smith, Kelly Gerling, Ph.D. NLP The New Technology of Achievement. Audiotapes. Chicago: Nightingale Conant
[iii] Anthony Robbins. Unlimited Power. Ballantine Books, Div. of Random House, 1986.
[iv] Paul Martin, M.D., The Healing Mind, the Vital Links between Brain and Behavior, Immunity and Disease. New York: St. Martin's Press, 1998.
[v] Deepak Chopra, M.D. Ageless Body, Timeless Mind. New York: Random House, 1993.

Chapter 7

Empowering Meaning to Any Event

Victor E. Frankl in his book Man's Search for Meaning introduced the term "logotherapy." In this book, Dr. Frankl examined the horrors he had experienced in the Nazi concentration camp of Auschwitz.i He was faced with some of the most horrifying experiences any human may go through in life. After his house and belongings were confiscated, he was stripped naked, his body hair was removed, and he was deprived of food and water. He lived in constant fear of being killed in the gas chambers. He was often brutally beaten. The Nazis killed his father, mother, wife, brother, and other family members. Except for a sister, all his family perished in concentration camps. He was exposed to brutal conditions, including being exposed to cold without much clothing and getting only a bowl of watery soup and a piece of bread for a full day's meal. His book provides vivid details of the terror he and other Jews experienced.

I am not aware of any more terrifying human experience than his. How could he find life worth preserving? Dr. Frankl's book explains what helped him and a few others survive in the concentration camps. He developed logotherapy based upon his experiences and indicated that it was the meaning they attached to events which helped them survive. In any traumatic experience, when everything is snatched away what alone remains is the ability to choose and ascribe an empowering meaning to the awful circumstances.

Here is a set of wheels, a recipe, for dealing with most traumatic events, or so-called problematic events in life. **What helped Dr. Frankl**

and a few others survive was to give an empowering meaning to the most difficult and painful life events. It actually changed how their minds and bodies reacted to the horrifying events in the concentration camps. He mentions that there is a close connection between the state of mind of a man, his courage and hope, or the lack of them, and the state of the immunity of his body. If someone gives a disempowering meaning, or loses courage and hope, the body may well give out suddenly.

I have long studied various people who experienced traumatic life experiences. Let us look at some well-known examples. Our first example is "Mothers Against Drunk Driving" (MADD). What happened to this mother? Candy Lightner's thirteen-year-old daughter, Cari, was killed by a drunk driver who had been a repeat offender.iii Is this a painful traumatic event? Yes, it is! What did Ms. Lightner do? She asked herself what she could learn from this painful experience and use for the benefit of others. She gathered her strength to start an organization against drunk drivers in the United States in 1980. One person who faced a painful experience has now been able to make a difference in the lives of thousands. Mothers Against Drunk Driving began as a one-woman organization and has expanded to four hundred chapters in the United States and has now become an international organization.

A second example, Mahatma Gandhi, was called a derogatory name and thrown out of a train in South Africa because he was a colored person. It was a painful experience. It drove him to start a movement which spread from South Africa to India. One man made a decision that he was going to ask the British to leave India. The personal pain of his experience drove him to create a phenomenal result. He created a national movement which managed to kick the English out of India. This started a chain reaction in many countries where British colonists were forced to leave. You may remember the British Empire ruled many different parts of the world at the start of the twentieth century. There was a saying, "The sun never sets on the British empire."

EMPOWERING MEANING TO ANY EVENT

However, one man made a decision to remove the British from his country and succeeded in what many others considered an impossible goal.

I have been studying what makes people achieve phenomenal results in life and have developed a set of questions, which you can ask yourself when facing a problem or painful life experience. I believe Mahatma Gandhi, Martin Luther King, Jr., and Candy Lightner asked this set of questions and came up with answers which helped them to give new, empowering meanings to their painful life experiences, and gave them the strength to create phenomenal results. Anyone can ask these questions, and if you ask these questions, you may be amazed at the answers you get.

These questions are:
1. What can I learn from this experience?
2. How can I make use of this experience for others and myself?
3. How can I make use of this experience for mankind?

Asking and answering these questions will empower you as you face difficult problems, situations, and painful experiences in your life. This practice will make you more creative and provide a phenomenal strength to deal with life's problems. **You will realize that this strength is within you just as it is in everyone else.** The questions give you the tools to access it. Let us apply this to a few examples.

1. <u>Mothers Against Drunk Driving:</u> A mother was faced with the death of her daughter by a drunk driver. Let us ask those three questions and see the results.

<u>Question #1:</u> What can I learn from this experience?

<u>Answer:</u> Drunk driving kills innocent people and this needs to be stopped.

<u>Question #2:</u> How can I make use of this experience for myself and others?

Answer: I can teach people drunk driving kills innocent people, and start an organization against drunk drivers that will help reduce drunk driving.

Question #3: How can I make use of this experience for mankind?

Answer: I can start an organization against drunk driving nationwide which will decrease the innocent deaths of people and cause increased awareness about the devastation caused by drunk driving.

2. Let us examine the case of Mahatma Gandhi.

Question #1: What can I learn from this experience?

Answer: People should not treat others poorly because of their color or race.

Question #2: How can I make use of this experience for myself and others?

Answer: I will convey to the British that my fellow citizens and I need not have to tolerate inhumane treatment.

Question #3: How can I make use of this experience for mankind?

Answer: I will teach people that we can achieve freedom by non-violence and live a dignified life as our own masters.

3. Let us explore the case of Martin Luther King, Jr.

Question #1: What can I learn from this experience?

Answer: People should not discriminate because of color or race.

Question #2: How can I make use of this experience for myself and others?

Answer: I will start a movement to end inequality.

Question #3: How can I make use of this experience for mankind?

Answer: I will teach people to treat every human being with equality and respect, and not as servants or lesser beings.

4. Let us examine the case of Mother Teresa who experienced so much human suffering and whose caring touched the entire world.

Question #1: What can I learn from this experience?

EMPOWERING MEANING TO ANY EVENT

<u>Answer:</u> People should not have to suffer because of hunger and no access to medical care.

<u>Question #2:</u> How can I make use of this experience for myself and others?

<u>Answer:</u> I will start an organization to help the poor and people who suffer living without dignity.

<u>Question #3:</u> How can I make use of this experience for mankind?

<u>Answer:</u> I will teach people to treat every human being with love, to share and to care for each other.

One can apply these questions to every leader in history who helped mankind, and realize by their actions that they may have asked similar questions in their minds, arriving at similar answers. You can use these questions whenever you are faced with problems, difficulties in life, or painful experiences. This system will give creative answers to your situation and put you in an empowering state. These questions will help one to give an empowering meaning to any painful experience.

Let us look at how some of the Vietnam War veterans in my seminars have responded to these questions. Vietnam War veterans have gone through the horrors and chaos of war, including seeing their friends being killed, not knowing who their enemy is, being treated with indignity when they returned from Vietnam, seeing violence first hand in their life, losing their families due to violence, and succumbing to alcohol and drug abuse which they used to numb their emotional pain. They have learned the Vietnam War wasted billions of dollars and untold energy and resulted in sufferings for them, their families and the Vietnamese themselves and solved no problems. Only a Vietnam War veteran will be able to explain the magnitude of problems caused by the war in Southeast Asia. One Vietnam veteran commented, "We can teach others, the young children, that violence does not solve problems, it increases problems. Do not use drugs and alcohol to deal with emotional pain, it will intensify your problems." He feels that the veterans can teach children in their neighborhoods the importance of non-violence.

We can look into how many top world leaders faced problems and painful experiences in their lives and examine what drove them to create change in the world. They asked empowering questions to tap into empowering answers within themselves. Learn to ask empowering questions; your brain will give empowering meaning to events, circumstances, and life experiences. You can create a set of empowering questions to help you find answers and have empowering feelings quickly, as opposed to letting yourself enter a disempowering state.

Empowering meanings create an empowering state of mind.

Let us look at another example. Paul and Robert, who are brothers, go to Six Flags, an amusement park. Paul loves and enjoys going on roller coaster rides. He feels joyous and excited after taking a roller coaster ride and he always wants to go back on the roller coaster. On the other hand his brother Robert feels anxious, nervous, and sick to his stomach when he takes a roller coaster ride. He feels like he's dying when he rides the roller coaster. When Paul feels joyous and excited, it is not only happening in his head but all over his body. When this happens, psychoneuroimmunologists have been able to demonstrate that Paul secretes interferon and interleukin-two substances which are protective to the body.iv On the other hand, when Robert rides the roller coaster, he is secreting adrenaline, cortisol and other substances which are damaging to his body.

Just imagine how you feel in your stomach and heart when you have a fearful response to any event versus when you feel joyous. Two brothers who grew up in the same household have different responses to the same roller coaster ride. One feels joyous and the other feels frightened and nervous, and this is happening not only in their heads but all over their bodies. Why is there this difference? The difference is due to them linking different meanings to the same event of riding a roller coaster.

Another brief example of this is someone who enjoys ocean waves and surfing, while another person is deathly afraid and gets anxious from the same ocean waves and wants to run away. The difference is due to them linking different meanings to the same experience of ocean waves. Now visualize what will happen if you continue having fearful responses on a chronic basis, in the case of phobias (fear of elevators, fear of being in crowded places, etc.). If you link disempowering meanings to any event, it will affect you not only in your head, but all over your body. Why not learn to give empowering meaning to any event to help you succeed in life?

For example, if one gives disempowering meaning to daily work because one believes in TGIF or that rainy/cloudy days are crummy days, imagine what will happen to their body chemistry? If they continue this disempowering meaning of "work sucks and I only live for Fridays," they are suffering five out of seven days a week. People try to run away from problems thinking they will go away, but why not solve these problems within us. I knew a person who kept running away from elevators because of his phobia, thinking it would go away, but unfortunately the phobia continued to spread to other areas like crowded places, enclosed places, movie theaters, amusement parks, etc. When people with TGIF syndrome perceive stress due to work during weekdays, their perception will affect them adversely. Stress can be induced by disempowering meanings linked to events, objects, etc.

Psychoneuroimmunologists have been studying the effects of stress on the immune system. Robert Ader from the University of Rochester Medical Center has done extensive research in this field. The psychoneuroimmunology field suggests a strong correlation between psychosocial factors and immune functioning. There has been evidence that a person's daily perceived stresses and current circumstances influence the central nervous system, which can adversely affect immune functioning. Many studies show the negative effects of stress on immunity and autoimmune disorders.v There has been evidence that the immune system and nervous system speak the same language. Immune system cells use chemicals called interleukins and interferons to communicate with each other. The same chemicals can also trigger receptors in the brain. Many substances of abuse including alcohol, cocaine, marijuana, heroin, and nicotine have been shown to suppress the immune system.

It is up to you to give whatever meaning you want to any event. Instead of allowing advertising commercials or something else to link these meanings in your brain, causing you to be in disempowering states, you can take charge of linking an empowering meaning to any event. Choose the meaning you wish to link to any event or object then check to see if it falls into the category of Actions for Success or Actions for Improvement. If your meaning falls into one of these two categories, you are on the path to success.

In the previous chapter we have learned that advertisers link the feelings of pleasure and significance to buying their products by conditioning your mind. It is so easily done. Beer companies, cigarette merchants, fast food restaurants and many other companies link the meanings of pleasure, relaxation, convenience, and fun to their products in order to make profits for themselves. However, the meaning they link in your mind is disempowering to you and your fellow human beings. For example, children and young adults have been made to believe they have to buy brand-name shoes to feel cool, great, super, strong and to perform great athletically. When children believe this, they are prisoners of their own desire of having those shoes. Their self-esteem derives from wearing certain shoes and not from within themselves.

EMPOWERING MEANING TO ANY EVENT

They live in fear of how people will perceive them if they do not have brand-name shoes; their self-worth is derived from a pair of brand-name shoes. Their feeling of self-worth can be lost if they do not have the brand-name shoes, and they are prisoners of the perceptions of others. When they cannot afford those shoes, they feel terrible about themselves. What do they do about it? They rob someone or shoot someone for the pair of shoes! This actually happens from time to time, especially in the urban areas of the United States.

Another example of this is when kids' minds are conditioned to having self-worth only if they have a certain brand-name jacket. Now ask yourself if this is an empowering meaning: "I have to have Brand X shoes to feel great. I live in fear of the perceptions of others, and my self-worth comes from what I am wearing and not from within myself." Watch any commercial with a critical eye, and you will be surprised at what they make us believe. A woman must shop in a certain location and have a shopping center "quickie" to feel good; she must have brand-name items to make her feel important, and so on. Once these meanings are linked in our brains we go on autopilot and we believe it is real. This is no different from a Vietnam veteran feeling sad or depressed when it rains, or getting anxious when the Fourth of July fireworks display begins.

When we live with these disempowering meanings in our brain, we are actually living in the bondage of fear of how people will perceive us if we lack brand-name items. This can explain the hundreds of items we end up buying to please others, and our living in fear of how others will perceive us without these brand-name items. I remember seeing a woman who constantly changed her hair color every few weeks based upon the preference of each new boyfriend. She worried each time if her new boyfriend would like her hair color, her lipstick, etc.-worrying that otherwise he would dump her. Her feelings of self-worth came from her hair color, which obviously did not last a long time. What a way to live life!

When we start with the disempowering meaning of the TGIF syndrome who is hurting? Who feels lousy, who feels frustrated? Who feels depressed? The TGIF advertisers? You will never see nature get upset if you continue to gripe about what a lousy, crummy, rainy day it is. You are the one who gets upset, irritable, frustrated, and sad and then takes it out on someone else. You may even end up seeing a psychiatrist due to this chronic, disempowering belief. The treatment for those frustrated, angry, sad feelings is usually a prescription for just a few hundred dollars more. Who loses again and starts the chain reactions of problems we describe in Chapter 13?

It will be best for us to learn to give an empowering meaning to events, a meaning which puts us in an empowering state and make us feel good, relaxed, happy, and joyous without using pills or drugs or alcohol. What if we say to ourselves, " Nature is doing its job, there is no point fighting it. I will accept the current weather and prepare to go on with my day." You will learn the recipe in Chapter 17 of how some people live longer, happily and healthily past the age of one hundred. They do not fight with the weather. They go about their business, regardless of whether it rains, or snows, or the sun shines. They do not get aggravated and cause *STRESS* to themselves. It is better to learn the recipe from them instead of being on a bunch of pills, or drinking alcohol or using recreation and street drugs to feel good.

Stress has become a household word in everyone's life.
What is stress?

Imagine if you ran into a car and have a head-on collision. What would you and the other person feel when you came out of your cars? Most people will reply, "We would be very angry or frightened and stressed-out." Dr. Robert Eliot, a Colorado cardiovascular researcher was traveling in Riyadh in the Middle East.vi He saw two Arabs, each driving a Mercedes Benz, crash into each other in downtown Riyadh.

EMPOWERING MEANING TO ANY EVENT

The two men were uninjured. They jumped out of their cars and began laughing and hugging each other. Most people would expect these two men to be stressed-out and screaming at each other. To the surprise of Dr. Eliot, these two men were hugging each other and laughing! The American visitor could not resist asking the interpreter what the men were talking to each other about and why they were laughing and hugging. The interpreter explained that the two men were thanking God (Allah) for the chance to meet each other this way.

The examples given earlier in this chapter and in Chapter 6, about the two brothers who reacted exactly the opposite about riding the roller coaster and the two friends who reacted quite differently when at the oceanfront, clearly demonstrate that the way you perceive events and the meanings you give to them will determine if you will feel stress and anxiety or joy and happiness. One cannot change the event, but one does have the choice to give an empowering meaning to it. The best example I have come across is the one I mentioned at the beginning of this chapter, Dr. Victor Frankl, who went through the horrifying events in the Nazi concentration camps. He relates in his book how people survived the daily horrifying experiences, including the threat of death on an ongoing basis, by the empowering meaning they gave to the events.

Most therapist and treatment modalities in psychiatry and psychology, or any counseling, are geared toward altering the meaning of traumatic events or painful experiences. I have yet to see anyone change his or her past. However, one can choose to give an empowering meaning to past or current painful experiences. This book describes several techniques for quickly linking an empowering meaning to any event.

If you give disempowering meaning to an event you will feel stress. Time magazine once published figures from the American Institute of Stress, which indicated 90 percent of all Americans feel highly stressed one to two times a week. According to another survey, 57 percent of

American women felt stressed most of the time. Stress costs billions of dollars to the American economy due to increased usage of the health care systems. One needs to understand that stress affects us physically, emotionally, and then in all other areas of life. If one wants to create a phenomenal success in life, he or she needs to master reducing the perceived stress. As I said earlier, one cannot change the event, but one can change the meaning attached to any event.

Let me expand on how stress may affect us. Stress and psychoneuroimmunology is a growing field. Description of it here is beyond the scope of this book but there are several books on the subject (see the Bibliography).

Stress causes an automatic biological response to demands made upon a person. It initiates a complex biochemical and biological process. The process may begin in the brain, and spread through the autonomic nervous system, releasing hormones and affecting the immune system. Both the nervous system and the endocrine system are involved, causing a series of reactions throughout the body.vii Stress can be divided into good stress (eustress), and bad stress (distress). People who perceive positive stress may lead productive lives. This book will focus on perceived bad stress (distress) and its effect on us.

Stress can be physical or psychological. Physical stress can be caused by environmental factors like extreme cold or heat, noise, physical injury, illness, electric shock, surgery, etc. Psychological stress can be caused by our attitude and the way we react toward threats from our environment. These threats can be imagined such as phobias of close places or elevators, or they can be real as in armed robbery. Psychosocial stress can be caused by interpersonal conflicts in relationships with one's spouse, employers, family members, neighbors, strangers, etc.

EMPOWERING MEANING TO ANY EVENT

When faced with stress it may affect us in the following ways:

1. Our adrenal glands will start secreting glucocorticoid hormones. These hormones are essential for metabolism of glucose in the right amount. However, under stress the excessive secretion can cause impairment in the immune system and make the body susceptible to illness and disease. The adrenal glands secrete cortisol, cortisone, and catecholamines. Too much of these hormones will decrease the body's resistance to infections, illness, and cancer due to resultant poor immune response.viii

2. The hypothalamus secretes endorphins, which are powerful natural painkillers. These are useful in the right amount. But chronic stress causes depletion of endorphins, which can aggravate chronic pain syndromes like arthritis, backache, migraine headaches, etc. The hypothalamus under stress also secretes a Corticotrophin-releasing hormone (CRH). When CRH affects the midbrain, it can cause anxiety and physical stress response.

3. Under stress, the thyroid producing excess thyroid hormones may cause symptoms of nervousness, shakiness, insomnia, tiredness and, in some people, weight loss.

4. Stress can induce stomach cramping, nausea, diarrhea, abdominal uneasiness, and constipation. The mouth may get dry under stress.

5. Heartbeats: Stress can cause palpitations (heart beating faster) and an increase in blood pressure (which may cause a stroke or heart attack).

6. Stress may reduce progesterone (in females) and testosterone (in males), the sex hormones. This may cause sexual dysfunction, decreased libido, infertility, and difficulty reaching orgasm. Stress may precipitate menstrual irregularities and cramping in women.

7. Stress may release more cholesterol from the liver into the bloodstream. Combining this with the increase in blood pressure will lead to increased incidence of stroke and heart attack. Cardiovascular disorders are the number one cause of deaths in United States. It is no surprise that more people die on Monday morning because many people may perceive

returning to work as stressful.

8. Stress has been shown to reduce natural killer cell activity, decrease lymphoproliferative response and reduce cellular immune control.

9. Effects of stress on the brain: Stress causes increased secretion of cortisol and cortisone. Too much cortisol can cause stress-induced progressive nerve loss as proved by a study on rats conducted by Stanford University biologists.ix In as short a time as three weeks, excessive cortisol changes the nerve cells and branches in the hippocampus which mimics the loss of cells resulting from aging. Stress may actually intensify brain cell loss normally occurring during aging. New York researchers suggest that stress can actually play a role in the development and worsening of Alzheimer's disease.x

Stress induces numerous physiochemical responses in the body. Stress affects the endocrine system, gastrointestinal system, cardiovascular system, immune system, and our nutrition. It may increase the incidence of cancer. Stress has been associated with the following list of conditions. The list is not complete because, as I have said earlier, the body/mind connection and psychoneuroimmunology constitute a vast area. **Most disorders are multifactorial.**

1. Allergies; asthma
2. Increased blood pressure
3. Angina; heart disease
4. Back pain; muscle spasms
5. Arthritis
6. Headaches
7. Gastrointestinal symptoms, including stomach ulcers and irritable bowel syndrome
8. Sexual dysfunction, including menstrual irregularities and pain in genitourinary organs
9. Increased proneness to cancer

EMPOWERING MEANING TO ANY EVENT

10. Increased susceptibility to infections; colds
11. Hair and scalp problems
12. Worsening of diabetes
13. Insomnia
14. Worsening of psychiatric illnesses, including depression and anxiety disorders
15. Problems related to infertility
16. Increased use of drugs and alcohol
17. Weight gain; weight loss
18. Proneness to accident
19. Poor work performance; poor attention span

Any of the above problems will start snowballing and causing problems in other areas of life affecting relationships, financial status, work, physical health, and spirituality. I do want to emphasize that it is essential for all of us to learn to master the interpretation of the meanings of events. If you want to succeed in life and create phenomenal results, learn to master the meanings of events. This will definitely help you cope with so-called "perceived stress." The people in our examples who succeeded the most were faced with more problems or so called "stressful events." The difference between the successful people and the others, is that most successful people learned to master the meanings they assigned to problematic events like rejection and failure. If you want to succeed in any area of life, do not reinvent the wheel: master linking empowering meaning to every event. Problems and difficulties are going to be part of life and they give us opportunities to grow. What makes you successful? It is your way of coping with the problems.

Find an empowering meaning to your life, a meaning which allows you to tap into your deepest potential, that source of unlimited success and energy that resides within you. Find a meaning which is empowering to yourself and fellow human beings and one which

HEMANT THAKUR, MD

will not hurt anyone else or planet Earth.

> *He who has a 'why' to live can bear almost any 'how.'*
> (Nietzsche)

---

[i] Victor E. Frankl. Man's Search for Meaning: An Introduction to Logotherapy. Boston: Beacon Press, 1984.
[ii] See note i above.
[iii] Information provided by Mothers Against Drunk Driving.
[iv] Deepak Chopra. Ageless Body, Timeless Mind. New York: Harmony Books, 1993.
[v] Robert Ader, David L. Felten, Nicholas Cohen. Psychoneuroimmunology. New York: Academic Press, 1991.
[vi] Brent Q. Hafen, Keith J. Karren. Kathryn J. Frandsen, N. Lee Smith. Mind Body Health: The Effects of Attitudes, Emotions and Relationships. Boston: Allyn and Bacon , a Simon & Schuster Company, 1996.
[vii] Paul Martin, M.D. The Healing Mind, the Vital Links between Brain and Behavior, Immunity and Disease. New York: St. Martin's Press, 1998.
[viii] See note vi above.
[ix] Bruce S. McEwen, "Hormones and the Nervous System," Advances 7(1) :1990: 50-54
[x] See note ix above.

Chapter 8

State of Mind

Emotions drive human behavior not the intellect. Here is a recipe we can learn by watching Martin Luther King, Jr., or Mahatma Gandhi or any leader in the world. If you watch them closely, you will realize they generate emotions in people's minds that cause them to take actions. I watched a videotape of one of the speeches of Dr. Martin Luther King, Jr. He displays powerful emotions in this speech. His words were, "I have a dream." If you watch it carefully you will notice his body gestures, his thundering voice, and his upraised hands were transmitting powerful emotions that caused thousands of people to take action.

A lot of doctors, psychologists, and PhDs have plenty of knowledge but they fail to take action and produce results. Many people have wonderful ideas but fail to take action. For example, why do people overeat, drink, do drugs, smoke, or even get involved in promiscuous relationships? It is due to their emotions. At an emotional level they are feeling uncomfortable, empty, nervous, anxious, or bored, which drives them to take actions and some of those actions may be disastrous. Take any human behavior: it can be constructive or destructive, empowering or disempowering; it is still driven by the emotions. The emotions drive human behavior. Emotions are nothing but a state of mind. Most of the time, the state of mind is at the mercy of past conditioning. Advertisers have linked that if you want to relax, drink my wine. If you want to have fun (a state of mind), drink my beer. If you are a youngster and you want to feel you are grown up, or feel you are cool, smoke my cigarettes. If you want to feel beautiful, have a haircut from a certain hairdresser.

We are wandering through different emotions triggered by various stimuli pushing our buttons (triggers), and we do not even realize it most of the time. For example, if a man accidentally listens to an certain old country love song, he starts thinking about a past relationship and the time he spent with his girlfriend on the lake. Or a woman might smell a certain perfume while walking in the mall and start to think of an old boyfriend. When I see a lobster in a grocery store it reminds me of spending time at my grandmother's house at the ocean, watching fishermen close by. Any of our five senses may trigger different memories and different emotions.

Common Destructive Behaviors	Connected to some type of uncomfortable feeling within self. (Do not feel good inside)
Smoking	Feels anxious, nervous, stressed, bored
Drinking an excess of alochol	Feels anxious, stressed, bored, lonely, depressed, fearful
Eating excessively	Feels anxious, nervous, stressed, bored, depressed
Shopping excessively	Feels anxious, nervous, stressed, bored, low self-esteem
Promiscuous sex	Feels anxious, nervous, stressed, bored, lonely, low self-worth
Watching excessive television	Feels anxious, nervous, stressed, bored, lonely, empty
Using street drugs	Feels anxious, nervous, stressed, bored, depressed, fearful

STATE OF MIND

If you manage your emotions instantaneously it will help you manage your behavior. For example if you feel nervous or anxious, you may start overeating. If you manage to change your nervousness instantaneously it will help you not to overeat. If you feel empty or bored, you may end up in a promiscuous sexual relationship. If you master changing that empty, bored feeling instantaneously you would not be engaging in a promiscuous sexual relationship. If you do not feel good about yourself and feel that you are not having pleasure, you may shop excessively. If you master creating pleasure, and can feel good about yourself instantly, it will help you to stop shopping excessively. Quickly managing our emotions or state of mind will help us to be successful.

Let me explain this step by step. Our behavior influences how other people behave towards us. For example, if I am angry and I start cursing you, waving my fist, pacing and stomping, how will you react? You may feel anxious, afraid, and angry or want to fight back. If I approach you in pleasant way, with a smile on my face, greeting you and wishing you to have wonderful day, how will you respond? You will respond differently because my behavior and gestures will have influenced your behavior. Another example of this is, if I come to an information desk at the hospital or any other business and approach the receptionist with anger, hostility, cursing and being demanding, how will he or she respond? Does this person want to be helpful to me willingly and pleasantly? No, probably not. On the other hand, if I approach the same person smiling and with a nice greeting, saying, "You have a beautiful smile," and ask her if she can help me, how will she react? She will want to cooperate and help me find what I am looking for. Thus, my behavior and gestures can influence other people's behavior. This is demonstrated by the following diagram:

My Attitude (State of Mind)   **Response of Other Person**
1. Approach with anger, hostility   Others may feel angry, hostile
2. Approach with fear, bitterness   Others feel anxious, nervous

3. Approach with paranoia, suspiciousness	Others may feel on edge, uncomfortable, worried
4. Approach with calm, peacefulness	Others may feel relaxed and serene
5. Approach with smile, cheerfulness	Others may feel cheerful, and smile at you
6. Approach with high energy, confidence	Others may feel your high energy and respect you
7. Approach with superior attitude	Others may feel you are snobbish

We can describe many other approaches and how they will influence other people's behavior towards you. There is one exception and this is the other **person's own internal conditioned perception of himself/herself and the conditioned perception of their surroundings based on this perception.** We will discuss this later. So far you have learned how your behavior will influence the behavior of others.

Now let us look at how our behavior may change based upon our own state of mind. If I feel happy, I will respond happily and will feel that the world is wonderful. If I feel life is full of opportunities and joy, I will be more optimistic. If I feel angry, irritable and unhappy, I will perceive and focus on how everything is not working well and on how people are not treating me well. Maybe they are mean to me and perhaps they mistreat me. You have heard the concept that if I am happy; I look at a half-glass of milk as being half-full. If I am unhappy, irritable, and angry, I will perceive that the glass is half-empty and that I do not have very much. Here is another example, which I use in seminars: If I feel I have been treated badly and I think that people do not like me because of my accent, my color, or my clothing, I will start gathering evidence to support this. If I feel suspicious and paranoid, I will look at the world suspiciously. Thus my own internal perception dictates how I feel. This is shown by the following diagram.

STATE OF MIND

My Internal Perception ➤	My State of Mind
1. I do not feel good about myself; I doubt myself.	I feel suspicious and feel people do not like me.
2. I perceive self-confidence and integrity within me.	I feel energetic, enthusiastic, and cheerful.
3. I feel weekdays suck TGIF is my way of life.	I feel irritable, angry, and and frustrated on weekdays.
4. I perceive every day as a great day (recipe of people who live longer, healthier lives)	I feel happy and energetic every day.
5. I feel people like me only if I have brand-name clothes and shoes.	I do not feel good if I am not wearing the brand-name clothes.
6. As a veteran, I feel door slamming is gunfire.	I become anxious, hyper-alert when door slams.
7. As a vietnam veteran at July 4th fireworks.	I feel frightened, nervous.
8. I perceive cigarette smoking as cool.	I feel relaxed while smoking.
9. Suicide bombing will give me ultimate honor.	As a Kamikaze I feel pleasure and honor while killing self by suicide bombing.
10 I perceive marriage as a loss of freedom.	I feel irritable, angry, unhappy in marriage.
11. I perceive marriage is a union of two people which is ultimate pleasure.	I feel pleasure being married.

By this time you will understand that your conditioned perceptions can create different states of mind from the same stimulus/trigger/anchor.

So far we have learned that our internal conditioned perceptions will govern our state of mind, which in turn influences our behavior, thus influencing the behavior of others. This is shown in the following diagram:

Our internal conditioned perception ➤ Our state of mind ➤ Influence others' behavior

One of the quickest ways to change your state of mind is by changing your body posture. This includes your breathing pattern, how you stand or sit, how you hold your shoulders, your facial expression, how you move your body and how you hold different muscles. For example, take a picture from Sports Illustrated magazine of a person who just won a championship. Stand exactly the way he or she is standing: the exact body posture including the face, neck, shoulders, arms, back, abdomen, and the lower body and legs. Hold it for just two to three minutes and see how you feel. You realize that changing your overall body posture and breathing quickly changes your state of mind. Find several pictures of people who are enthused, and try to duplicate their posture for just a few minutes. You will notice that you feel differently and probably you feel the same emotions as the person in the picture. On the other hand, if you look at a picture of a depressed person, and mimic the exact body posture of the depressed person, breathing the way he breathes, and visualizing similar ideas in your mind, you will start to feel unmotivated, depressed, and sad. A depressed person sits in a slumped position, face drooped, neck tilted down, and shoulders slumped. The person is breathing shallowly, and sitting in the fetal position. Just changing your body posture will immediately change your state of mind. This may sound ridiculous, but it works in minutes. As long as you are holding the posture, for example, of a person who feels victorious and joyous, you will feel joyous. The trick is how to continue this without effort. We will study this more later in the book. So far we have learned that if we change our posture it will change our state of mind instantaneously without taking a pill or drug. This is explained by the following diagram.

Our body posture/physiology ⟶ Our state of mind

Wouldn't it be nice if we can hold our body posture in a certain way and change our state of mind without effort? We have already learned how to create conditioned responses (Chapter 6) and link them to triggers or anchors. For example, we learned how to access a state of joy in few

STATE OF MIND

seconds when we have already linked our joyful state to a trigger. Remember the example of Perry who linked rubbing his chin to joyful state or the veteran who linked rubbing his forefingers to feeling peaceful? If you want to feel joyful or romantic when going on a date, all you have to do is push your trigger. This will cause a chain reaction changing your state of mind and thus your behavior and thus influence your date's behavior. The following diagram illustrates this:

Push your trigger → Instant change in state of mind → Change own behavior → Influence others' behavior

Now let us see what fireworks do to a Vietnam War veteran on the Fourth of July. Let us learn how this works and see how we can use this to benefit us in many areas of life. This happens in a few seconds without any effort or planning. Even though this is a disempowering experience, we all can learn how this can work in a few seconds to change our state of mind and behavior. Then we will study how this can be used beneficially to create a positive state of mind and positive behavior instantaneously.

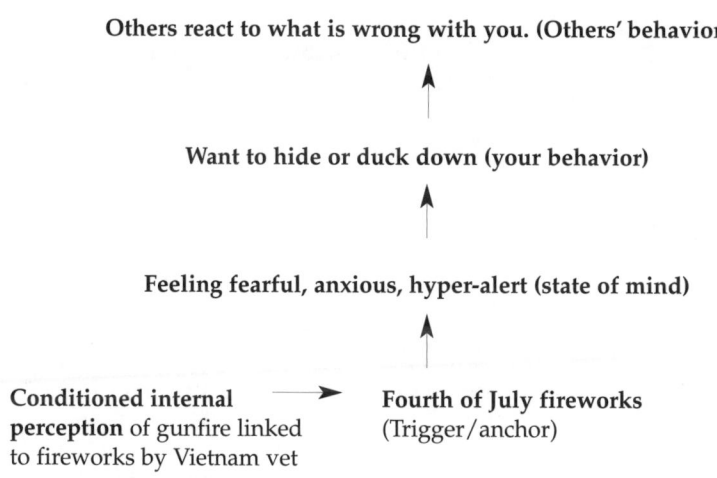

Others react to what is wrong with you. (Others' behavior)
↑
Want to hide or duck down (your behavior)
↑
Feeling fearful, anxious, hyper-alert (state of mind)
↑
Conditioned internal perception of gunfire linked to fireworks by Vietnam vet → **Fourth of July fireworks** (Trigger/anchor)

Reaction of Vietnam Veteran to Fourth of July Fireworks

This is very similar to when you are driving your car and you see red and blue flashing lights in the rearview mirror. When this happens, most drivers instantly worry that they have violated a traffic law or have faulty equipment. The red and blue flashing lights trigger the anxious feelings in you. You instantly feel fearful and anxious and your state of mind is hyper-alert.

Let us take another example, which has been mentioned previously and is very popular in my seminars: the TGIF syndrome. People who live their lives in the TGIF syndrome have a conditioned internal perception that they only live for weekend parties and that work sucks. It is interesting to see how the trigger of a workday will cause a chain reaction of disempowering behavior in people with the **TGIF belief system**. When I showed this to my audience, including some who used to live the TGIF life, they laughed at their own past behavior when they realized how their minds were conditioned.

Boss chewing you out (other's behavior)
↑
Not doing your job (own behavior)
↑
Feeling irritable; poor attitude (state of mind)
↑
Conditioned internal perception ⟶ **Workday (Trigger)**
of TGIF and "work sucks"

Once you understand and practice this technique, you can use to create many empowering responses and behaviors. Let us use this concept in a way that is empowering for all of us. Say I have linked a trigger to feeling energetic. I come home and push the trigger, it will put me in an energetic state and I can spend time with my spouse and children in an energetic way. The following diagram illustrates this.

STATE OF MIND

Wife and kids treat me nicely (others' behavior)
↑
I spend time with wife and kids with enthusiasm (own behavior)
↑
Feeling energetic (state of mind)
↑
Conditioned internal perception ⟶ Push your own trigger
that spending time with family
is ultimate joy

We can use this technique in many areas. After frequent repetitions it will become a conditioned response and it will be easier to trigger an empowering state of mind by pushing the trigger and thus creating empowering behavior. Now let us use this in areas to replace destructive behavior. So far we have studied that when people engage in any destructive habit like excessive eating, smoking, drinking, using drugs, excessive shopping, or promiscuous sex, it is because the person engaging in the behavior has been feeling distressed, uncomfortable bored, empty, lonely, irritable, anxious, nervous, or sad. If the person can change his state of mind instantly, in a few seconds, before he reaches the bar, takes the drugs, or eats the huge meal; it will help him to stop the destructive behavior. For example when you feel nervous within, you overeat. If you push your trigger it will change your state of mind to positive, creating an empowering state and if you no longer feel nervous, this will help you not to overeat. This can be used in areas like smoking, drinking excessively, using drugs, excessive shopping, or promiscuous sex, to decrease these kinds of behaviors. After repeated practice, all you have to do is to push the trigger, which will cause an empowering response in a few seconds without a conscious effort.

We learned in this chapter:

1. Our behavior influences how other people behave towards us.
2. My own state of mind determines my behavior.

3. My internal conditioned perceptions may determine my behavior and emotions.
4. Others' conditioned perceptions may determine their behavior and emotions.
5. My body posture and body physiology can rapidly change my state of mind.
6. Pushing my triggers will rapidly change my state of mind and body physiology.

> *I no longer try to change outer things. They are simply a reflection.*
> *I change my inner perception and the outer reveals the beauty so long obscured by my own attitude. I concentrate on my inner vision and find my outer view transformed. I find myself attuned to the grandeur of life and in unison with the perfect order of the universe.*
> (Daily Word)

Chapter 9

Emotional Record

Have you observed how you react when you are angry with your spouse? If you study your pattern of expressing anger, you will realize you have a certain sequence of using body gestures, certain words, and certain interactions in a certain succession, and then speaking with anger. If you videotaped different times when you were angry, and replayed this videotape, you would be amazed at how you have a consistent pattern of expressing anger. Just think about your spouse, and you will realize that he or she has a certain pattern of expressing emotions. It can be anger, joy, seduction, frustration or any other emotion. You can almost sense how he or she is going to react once you push his or her trigger or button. I remember I used to have a certain sequence or pattern of expressing my anger by pouting and saying, "There is nothing wrong." If you replayed how you expressed anger a few weeks ago and compared it to a recording of how you expressed it three or four years ago, you would realize that there is a pattern with a sequence, which becomes a sequential ceremony. It is like the old plastic records we used to play. They played the same song every time once you put the needle in the right groove on the edge of the record.

This sequential ceremony applies to any emotional response you may have. It can be happiness, joy, peacefulness, arousal, anger, or sadness. Take the example of arousal and being seductive. Each of us has a certain sequential pattern of expressing seductiveness, which differs from one individual to another, but will remain the same in each individual. Now imagine the analogy of playing the plastic record after putting the needle in the groove at the edge. It will play the same song every time. Then imagine what would happen if you scratched the record with some sharp object back and forth. Can you play the same song? Once the record has been scratched, you donít want to play the same song because you will hear a garbled sound. You have seen this in the past when you accidentally scratched a record. If you scratch the emotional record, you will not want to play the same emotional song. We can use this concept to scratch out old emotional disempowering records, while we still preserve the empowering records. How do we do this? The technique is similar to scratching the plastic record and destroying the old song.

For example, my ex-girlfriend started arguing with me after a trigger of remembering past disputes. I sensed that she was going to get exceedingly angry and play the old song of blame, and end up spoiling the evening. Unless I interrupted her pattern of behavior she would continue to play the old record once the trigger was pushed. What I did in this case was to remember an event which she had shared with me that she found extremely funny. I suddenly brought up this story of her seeing a little mouse in her apartment and how she initially perceived that she was seeing something moving around from the corner of her eye, while she was reading a book. She then started feeling that she was seeing things and something was wrong with her, until she finally saw the mouse and realized she was not hallucinating, and there was a real mouse in her apartment. She frantically called the apartment manager late at night to get rid of the mouse crying, "You have to save me from this mouse!" When she finally got rid of the mouse, she always thought it was very funny how she had imagined that she had been seeing things in her apartment. When I realized that she was starting to get angry, I suddenly said to her, "Remember the mouse in your apartment?" She broke into laughter, and forgot about getting angry. What happened here was that her pattern (record) was interrupted, due to being reminded of a crazy memory (which scratched the record) and she was unable to play her old repetitive song of anger.

EMOTIONAL RECORD

Let me give you another example. While running seminars for Vietnam War veterans, I realized that if someone talked long enough about the United States government, a particular Vietnam War veteran would begin to feel angry which would escalate to the point of him leaving the class. In this case talking about the government was a trigger similar to putting the needle to the edge of the old plastic record, which then will play the same old song. As I noticed him becoming angry, I sat across from him and reminded him of a funny incident described by another Vietnam War veteran just half an hour before, which had made everybody laugh uncontrollably. As he remembered the crazy incident he broke into laughter and forgot what was making him angry. There were a couple of things happening here. In this patient's case, talking about the government is a trigger leading to anger but the funny story was a trigger to making him laugh. This second trigger of the hilarious story interrupted his first record of anger and thus he could not play the old song; instead, he started laughing.

I met a colleague who said to me, "Hemant I am worried about these changes in the health care industry." I realized that usually when this particular woman would start on this topic, most of our other colleagues would support her worries, saying that they did not know where managed care was going to take them. They all ended up worrying and irritated. I stopped in front of her and said, "Can you show me what worry is? I need to learn that." She looked at me as if I were insane, but she did stop playing her record of worries.

Many times we keep repeating the memories of painful or distressing events in our minds literally hundreds of times. This creates emotional distress and pain, and wastes time and energy as we think about past events we cannot change. I have yet to see anyone who has managed to change their past events. The only change one can make is in the present moment. One way of interrupting your old disempowering emotional movie of distressing events or memories and replacing it with a new empowering movie in your mind, is to visualize your old pattern of disempowering beliefs as if you are running a videotape in your mind. For example, consider me having an argument with someone who cursed me and threatened me in public while he was intoxicated. This scenario started in a restaurant and ended up in the parking lot. When I came home, this event kept running through my mind again and again, bringing back the same distress I felt while going through the incident. I was playing this same scenario in my mind endlessly, causing myself distress and wasting my time. What could I do to interrupt this pattern?

Try this technique of "scratching the record" which works great. Visualize this whole scene as a videotaped movie, starting from the parking lot and going back to the restaurant. Run it backward and forward as fast as you can in your mind (as if you were rewinding and fast forwarding a videotaped movie). While doing this, make the person look silly, stupid, a slob, or picture him dropping his pants. Give him a visual picture which makes you laugh. It may be anything which is absolutely ridiculous, but not distressing to you. Repeat this movie of the event in your mind as fast as possible backward and forward. Then superimpose the stupid slob who was drooling from his nose and dropping his pants as he lost his belt, or something which will make you laugh. Repeat this for several minutes.

After a while try to visualize this distressing event in your mind. What you will find out is that you have the silly image and laughter coming to your mind or you will see a blurry non-distressing image. This technique may sound absolutely ridiculous and crazy, but it works. Try it; it does not cost you anything. You can do it on your own and you don't need to take a pill or a drink to decrease the distress associated with the event. NLP The New Technology of Achievement by Charles Faulkner describes and demonstrates many variations of this technique. These techniques are based upon how our brain erases some of our past experiences unknowingly. Do not reinvent the wheel. Use what your

EMOTIONAL RECORD

brain has already been doing successfully. Get charge of yourself and use the recipe to erase distressing pictures of past events.

Most of the memories we play in our mind have two components to them. One is imagery and the second is the emotions we have attached to it. Imagery has colors and sounds. For example, a person is threatened in an elevator at knifepoint and robbed. The victim feels the emotional distress of being anxious, frightened, violated, threatened, and humiliated. When he remembers the event he also experiences the same emotional distress of feeling anxious, frightened, violated, threatened, and humiliated for many hours. If you interrupt the imagery, it will decrease the emotional distress attached to it. Ask a Vietnam War veteran to show you how vivid memories and imagery of Vietnam bring back the same intensity of distress he felt during war.

The key point learned here is to break your old pattern by interruption, using something crazy, funny, or ridiculous as long as it is not harmful to you or anybody else. This will interrupt your old habits of disempowering reactions, or behavior. Unless you interrupt the old pattern, your mind will play the same old song and you will get the same results. Neuro-linguistic programming teaches various methods of pattern interruption.

The next thing to do is replace the old song with something new and empowering. If you repeat this numerous times and condition your mind it will become an automatic response. Commercials do this to us all the time and attach pleasurable responses to their product. Once your mind is conditioned you function on autopilot. An example of numerous conditioned responses is how you learn to drive a car. Driving a car is a very complex task. You want to leave your office, get to the parking lot, get into your car, and start driving home. While doing that, you go through numerous complex tasks without consciously thinking about them.

HEMANT THAKUR, MD

First you have to figure out how to get out of your office by accessing your memory to remember the way out. When you come to the door you have to figure out whether to push the door open or pull the door open. Then you have to figure out where your car is. When you get close to your car, you have to reach in your pocket and get the right key out for the car. Then you have to figure out which way to turn the car key to open the door. Then you get into your car and remember to put your seat belt on. These are just a few complex tasks that you do automatically without thinking because of repeated conditioning. Once you condition yourself by interrupting your old pattern and superimposing a new pattern, it will become an automatic response.

Interrupt your old disempowering records and stop playing the old disempowering emotional songs. Keep the empowering records and straighten them to play empowering emotional songs.

Attachment is the great fabricator of illusions:
reality can be attained only by someone who is detached.
(Simone Weil)

Charles Faulkner, Gerry Schmidt, Robert McDonald, Tim Hallbom, Suzi Smith, Kelly Gerling, Ph.D. NLP
The New Technology of Achievement. Audiotapes. Chicago: Nightingale Conant
Anthony Robbins. Unlimited Power. Ballantine Books, Division of Random House, 1986.

Chapter 10

Play a New Song

In the previous chapter we learned how to interrupt and stop playing the emotional memories of old songs again and again. What do we do now, with all the empty time this has created? Here is a recipe I learned while running an alcohol and drug rehabilitation program. It is a recipe Alcoholics Anonymous (AA) teaches in their programs. Stop playing the old record of previous behavior and replace it with new empowering behaviors, hobbies, and new friends. For example, a person was used to playing an old song of finishing his work every day, getting into his automobile, going down to a local bar with his buddies, and hanging around the bar till the late evening. If he wants to maintain sobriety, he must interrupt his old behavior and replace it with a new behavior. Otherwise he will go back to the same bar with the same buddies, stay out late in the evening, and even if he says he has the intention of not drinking, he will drink, because he has not replaced the old behavior with a new one.

Alcoholics Anonymous teaches people to change the pattern of their old behavior and replace it with a new behavior. In this case, the person who wants to maintain sobriety will need to find new friends and new hobbies to fill his evenings. Chapter 3, **Actions for Success**, will teach you how to choose a new behavior, a new pattern of thinking, new friends and new hobbies, which will lead to ultimate success for all. In the case of this man determined to stay sober, he needs to find hobbies where he can socialize with people who don't drink and still enjoy life. Instead of reaching for a can of beer, he needs to condition himself to reach for a glass of fresh juice, or a glass of milk or water. He needs to learn that instead of driving down to a local bar, he can go jogging with his wife down the local trail. Instead of sitting in the bar and gossiping, he can spend time learning something new which will make him grow and focus on new goals.

Alcoholics Anonymous teaches that if you hang around the old drinking buddies you are going to continue the old behavior of drinking because you are reconditioning your mind to the old behavior. If you continue taking old actions, and continue your old behavior, how will you create a change or a different future? Thus, it is very clear that if you want to create a better, brighter future you have to change your old patterns of thinking, old patterns of behavior, and old buddies. Let me restate, *one definition of insanity is to keep doing the same things and expecting different results*.

Let us take the example that you want to improve your energy level and maintain a normal body weight. You are used to stopping for fast food on your way home. You come home and devour that greasy food, reach for a soda pop and plop onto the sofa in front of the television for three or four hours where your only activity is pushing the remote control button to change channels. In the meantime, your spouse wants you to spend time with the family. Is this old behavior going to help you create energy, maintain a normal body weight, and have a better relationship with your family? You will have to interrupt this past behavior and replace it with a new empowering behavior. In this case, the new behavior may be going for a walk or a bike ride with your children around the neighborhood, observing nature and talking to your kids and spouse. Again what we are doing here is replacing the old behavior with a new pattern. If we do not change the old patterns, we will return to the same old results.

PLAY A NEW SONG

Let us take another example. If you are accustomed to running the same old negative thought patterns repeatedly in your mind-creating sadness, anxiety or some kind of distress-you need to interrupt this old disempowering pattern and replace it with a new empowering pattern of thinking. Someone has estimated that the human mind goes through sixty thousand thoughts a day. Out of this more than 90 percent are old memories, old patterns of thinking, or old behaviors. If we spend more than 90 percent of the time thinking about old information and continue old thinking patterns, how can we create a different future? We have to replace the old **disempowering** emotional records with new **empowering** ones and start playing a new song in our mind. Just imagine: if you continually play the old sad songs which constantly bring back the painful old memories and imageries in your mind, it continues to bring back the attached emotional distress. We have to start playing a new song, which will generate new feelings and new constructive patterns of behavior.

We need to condition these new patterns by repetition again and again until they become an automatic response. It is similar to how you learn the complex task of driving a car. Once you are conditioned to driving a manual transmission, you do not consciously think about pushing down on the clutch pedal, changing the gears or looking in the rearview and side mirrors while changing lanes. You do these things automatically because you have been conditioned. Think about your old behaviors, which used to be a conditioned response, because many times you have gotten into your automobile and driven down to the local bar for the evening, or returned home to spend the whole night in front of the television. You do not consciously think about these activities, you just end up doing them because you have conditioned responses.

You need to condition your new pattern until it becomes an automatic response. So instead of flopping onto the sofa, you jump onto a bicycle and ride on a bike trail or through your neighborhood. Instead of reaching for a fast-food meal, stop at a local grocery store and pick up something healthier and delicious to eat. Unless we replace the old disempowering behavior and emotional patterns, we will go back to the old pattern and old way of thinking. If your old behavior was helping you to relax, deal with stress, or socialize, you must find a new constructive behavior to achieve this. It is absolutely critical to do this. We also need to associate pleasure with the new behavior, and identify new empowering meaning with the event. This is explained in Chapter 4, **The Two Masters**.

The next part of the recipe learned from Alcoholics Anonymous is to recondition ourselves to this new behavior again and again otherwise we will relapse into the old behavior. Alcoholics Anonymous teaches that just because you went through a program once and learned a new behavior, it doesn't mean it is going to stay with you just because you have knowledge about it. They emphasize that one needs to recondition the new behavior and new patterns by attending AA meetings and having sponsors and having new friends who maintain a sober life. To maintain your new behavior and new patterns of thinking, you need to recondition your mind on a regular basis again and again. This is absolutely critical. Ask an alcoholic who has sobered up, and he will tell you that If you stop going to the AA meetings or stop communicating with your sponsor you will go back to the old pattern of behavior.

We can apply this to people who try to diet. People learn from various programs how to lose weight, but very often gain all the weight back, because they have failed to maintain and recondition the new pattern of behavior on a regular basis. Chapter 12, on how to lose and maintain weight, will give details on this concept related to weight reduction and maintenance. Set activities for yourself to condition yourself again and again on a regular basis. As you take each step, link it to pleasure, reward yourself, and give yourself a pat on the back to reinforce your new conditioned pattern. Remember your brain is always going to lead you toward

PLAY A NEW SONG

activities of avoiding pain and gaining pleasure. Positive reinforcement helps the brain avoid feeling bored with the new pattern of behavior.

Check to see if your new behavior is beneficial in all areas of life by asking the six simple questions you learned in Chapter 3, **Actions for Success**. Your new **empowering** pattern of thinking and behavior should be able to replace the old **disempowering** pattern of behavior in all areas of life. For example if your old behavior helped you socialize and have fun, the new behavior should help you to socialize and have more fun. If your old behavior helped you to relax and deal with stress, make sure your new behavior helps you to relieve stress, relax, lose weight and yet have pleasure. If you used to hang around with old buddies in a bar to gossip and make small talk for hours, then find new friends who enjoy a good conversation and with whom you can have fun and laugh and grow while discovering new things. If your old disempowering pattern of watching television helped you to relax, replace that with a new empowering pattern of exercising and watching an educational program on television, or spend time with your family doing some exciting hobbies. Learn to play a new empowering song in place of the old disempowering song.

> *Your vision will become clear only when you look into your own heart.*
> *Who looks outside, dreams, who looks inside, awakes.*
> (Carl Jung)

Chapter 11

FOCUS YOUR ATTENTION!

At any given moment the human mind is faced with thousands of stimuli. There is background noise and thousands of sights are within your view. Our minds process thousands of thoughts of what happened today, yesterday, a month ago, or even years ago. Our minds also wander with thoughts of the future, fantasies, and dreams.

How do you focus on only the empowering aspects of life? To answer this question, let me ask: what would you do if you wanted to find a certain program on a computer? You would look into specific files to find information about that particular topic. How would you find help on a computer? It is done by asking questions or clicking on a help icon. Your brain contains data from thousands of files. Whatever you concentrate on, you will visualize in your mind. Say you ask yourself the simple question, "What happened two hours ago?" Your brain will find answers to that question by checking all of the files. At that very moment your brain is focusing on events which occurred two hours ago. You know very well that you have stored the memories of thousands of hours in your brain. The moment you are focusing on a certain aspect of life or event, your mind will think about it.

How about if you ask the question, "Why don't I achieve the things I want to in my life?" Your brain will come up with an answer. Your brain will search for an answer in the stored files, and if it does not succeed in finding an answer it will make one up. On the other hand, what if you should ask, "How can I achieve this?" Your brain will look for answers, and produce them. You realize just by asking two different questions that you get two different responses. In the first example, you asked an irrelevant question and you got a disempowering answer. In the second example, you asked a specific, relevant question and you got an answer that will empower you.

Let us take another example. If I ask a question like "Why doesn't my boss notice what a good worker I am?" My brain will find an answer for that or make one up. Yet if I phrase the question, "What can I do so my boss realizes that I am a devoted worker," my brain will also come up with an answer for that. Here again the first question gives a disempowering answer. The second question provides an empowering answer. It is essential for us to learn to ask empowering questions, which result in empowering answers and motivates us. This also helps us in entering an empowering state. Empowering questions guide us toward finding solutions and make us feel energetic, powerful, grateful, and positive. Many teachers learn to ask strategic questions which get their students' attention; this in turn gets the students focused on the topic the teacher wants them to be focused on. This can also help the teacher to redirect the students' attention away from distractions.1

Let us not reinvent the wheel. As we pointed out earlier, consider certain world leaders and what they did when faced with problems. Mahatma Gandhi was called a derogatory name and thrown out of a train because he was a colored person. Most people would respond in this situation by asking a disempowering question, "Why are they treating me so badly? Poor me. The world is unfair to me." In this case your brain will come up with a disempowering answer and create the sense of a "poor me" feeling. Instead, Mahatma Gandhi asked questions like, "What can I learn from this? How can I change this for myself and for others? How can I change racial discrimination? How can I obtain freedom for my country through non-violent means?

FOCUS YOUR ATTENTION

How can I make use of this and serve humanity?" Questions like this led to Mahatma Gandhi's success. He found empowering answers. He learned that people should not discriminate against each other because of race, color, and religion. He came up with the answer, "I need to teach people not to discriminate against each other because of race, religion, or color, and to stop treating people as servants or lesser-beings because of their color." He used this to benefit humanity and mankind, create massive changes in the world, and obtain freedom for his country, using nonviolent means.

To highlight an example from earlier chapters, the woman who founded Mothers Against Drunk Driving (MADD) had a daughter who was killed by a drunk driver. She asked an empowering question to herself, "What can I learn from this and how can I make use of this to help others?" She came out with empowering answers and started an organization against drunk driving. She has been able to make a great difference in people's awareness about drunk driving and decrease the incidence of drunk driving fatalities.

Compare this to a woman I knew. She constantly kept asking questions such as, "Why did I grow up in a family with an alcoholic father who beat up my mother in front of me? Why did I grow up around convicts working on my father's farm? Why do I get sick all of the time?" It was no surprise that she kept finding disempowering answers and feeling depressed and getting into a frenzy about her past life. **I do not know anybody who can change his or her past.** I am sure, myself, that I cannot change my past. The only thing you can do is in the present moment. What you do in the present moment will create your future. Thoughts about the past and future are in your imagination. If you want to create a different and brighter future, you have to focus on new empowering questions, look at new ways of thinking, find empowering answers and take actions toward your goals.

This woman in the case above could have asked these empowering questions we learned in Chapter 7:

1. "What could I learn from my background?"
2. "How can I make use of this for myself and others?"
3. "How can I make use of these experiences for the benefit of humanity?"

If she had asked these questions, she would have come up with empowering answers and it would have put her in an empowering state. You have to learn to focus on empowering meanings and develop the habit of asking empowering questions. Asking these empowering questions allows you to enter an empowering state. Make a list of questions which will help you focus on the empowering aspects of life. Teachers often use these types of questions, to create empowering states in students. Make a list of empowering questions that will help you to pinpoint your talents, which can be beneficial to yourself and others. For example:

1. What is my natural talent? What is it that I am good at?
2. How can I make use of this for my family and myself?
3. How can I make use of this to create financial freedom?
4. How can I make use of my natural talent to benefit humanity?

Every human being has some natural talent, something they are able to do better than most others. One of the questions I frequently ask myself is: How can I make use of what I learn to help humanity?

As we discussed in Chapter 8, everyone knows the comparative concept of, "So if a glass is filled to midpoint, is it half-full or half-empty?" Whatever you focus on you will see. If you say the glass is half empty, you focus on the emptiness of the glass and similarly the emptiness of life. If you say the glass is half full, you are asking how you can enjoy it and make use of it. You focus on the fullness of the glass and similarly the fullness and happiness in life, which is positive and empow-

FOCUS YOUR ATTENTION

ering. Your mind is constantly evaluating various environmental and intellectual stimuli, various past and current experiences, and sensual stimulation. The evaluations of various stimuli and experiences are accomplished in your mind by asking questions. If you ask empowering questions, you get empowering answers. Ask "How can I do this; how can I enjoy facing this challenge?" and you will get empowering answers. You will feel great; you will feel empowered. If you ask "poor me" questions; "why do I get victimized" questions; you will get "poor me" answers.

Remember that your mind will see whatever you focus on. If you don't learn to focus on finding empowering meanings, your mind will roam and create waste. Learn to focus on empowering events and meanings on a consistent basis, which create an empowering state of mind and feelings. Another way you can improve your focus is through meditation which is discussed in Chapter 18.

Lesson learned in this chapter:

1. **Asking a strategic empowering question will help you focus on an empowering aspect of life and will create an empowering state.**
2. **If you ask a disempowering question, you will get a disempowering answer and create a disempowering state.**
3. **Ask questions to stimulate creative thinking. Ask questions that focus on "how" and "what," rather than "why." For instance, ask yourself how you can solve a challenging problem; how you can put yourself in a resourceful state; what is your greatest skill; and how can you make use of your greatest skill for yourself and others.**

A problem is a chance for you to do your best.
(Duke Ellington)

i Ronald T. Hyman. Strategic Questioning. Englewood Cliffs, N.J.: Prentice Hall, 1979. Focus Your Attention!

Chapter 12

Weight Reduction

So far we have learned so many different techniques. Let us see how they can be applied to weight reduction and later to any other goals we set up.

If a person who is overweight decides to lose weight, the first thing he or she needs to do is set up a goal. The goal should be precise and there should be a time limit for achieving the goal. For example, if I weigh two hundred pounds and I want to reduce my weight, my goal should read:

1. I will reduce from 200 pounds to 150 pounds.
2. I'll get this done in six months (give a specific date).

The next step to take is to start taking action toward reaching my goal. In this case my actions will begin with changing my eating habits. I must stop eating fattening snacks, fast food, and a diet high in fat and calories. I will begin eating healthy, 70 to 80 percent water-content foods. I need to specify some further actions, such as stopping at a grocery store to getting healthy food instead of my usual habit of stopping by a fast-food restaurant and buying a hamburger, fries, and soda. We learned in the first few chapters that you must take actions immediately which will signal your brain that you are creating success. Take daily, consistent actions and keep your goal in sight at all times. In this case, you can keep your goal in sight by taking a picture from a magazine of a person who looks like you would like to look. Stick that picture on a bathroom mirror and write on top of it, "I will look like this by December 24."

We need to look into what usually makes us procrastinate and not take actions, thereby continuing our old actions. For example, you may perceive that taking the action of stopping at a grocery store is more painful than just grabbing a quick hamburger, fries, and a soda, or that eating a sack of potato chips and drinking a six-pack in front of the television is very pleasurable. We learned in Chapter 4, **The Two Masters,** that every action we take is driven by trying to avoid some pain or discomfort and gain some pleasure or comfort. We learned that if we associate massive pain with the behavior we want to get rid of or avoid and associate pleasure with taking actions towards our goal, our brains will automatically continue taking those actions towards the goal. In the case of weight reduction, we need to link massive amounts of pain to our old patterns of eating behavior and a massive amount of pleasure to new, empowering behaviors and new actions, which will help us reduce our weight and create better health.

Let me give you an example of a friend of mine, Perry. In the past Perry used to go to the hamburger places for the usual hamburger, fries, and a soda. Over the years he had become overweight and hypertensive. He had been on medication for ten years. Perry attended one of my seminars and I asked him, "If you continue eating the way you are eating, what will happen?" He said, "I will get more overweight and continue to have high blood pressure." I told him this is just the beginning of the problem. I went on to explain that if he continues eating this way he will gain more weight. This excess weight is an extra burden on his body, on all of his weight-bearing joints, including his ankles, knees, and hip joints, and also on his back. Even his heart will be affected as it will have to supply blood to excess tissue in the body. It is similar to driving a one-ton truck with three-ton load on it. It will make the truck wear out more quickly.

I asked Perry if he would like to wear out his body by excess weight causing excess wear and tear on his joints, heart, lungs, muscles, and

WEIGHT REDUCTION

other body tissues. I said, "If you continue this you will be tired and fatigued when you come home and you will not have enough energy to spend time with your wife and children, or to pursue your hobbies. Your wife will not like seeing her husband always tired and not having enough energy to spend quality time with the family. You already have hypertension, and if you continue to gain weight your high blood pressure will continue to escalate."

Then I asked him, "Perry, what will happen if you continue to have high blood pressure?" He replied, "I may have a stroke or a heart attack."

At this point I said to him, "This is just the beginning of a series of other problems. When you have a heart attack, your wife will experience high anxiety and panic and call 9-1-1. Then you will have an ambulance coming to your door with blaring sirens and everyone in your neighborhood will be wondering what is happening at your home. The trouble has just begun Perry. You will be put on a stretcher by the paramedics, who will stick needles in your arms and tubes in your nose. They will put you in an ambulance and start driving back to the hospital. In the meantime, you will hear them talking via radio to the doctors in the Emergency Room about your condition. These doctors are ordering pokes with needles to give you more medication. Is this pleasure or pain?"

He replied, "That is painful."

I continued, "This is just the beginning of your trouble Perry. Then you come to the fancy Emergency Room where the resident doctors, medical students, respiratory therapists, nursing staff, EKG technicians, etc., will greet you. They all want to jump on you and find out what's wrong with you. They will ask you a bunch of questions and then say, 'Oh, yes . . . we must do some tests.' Just for a few thousand dollars. By the way, the ambulance bill for the trip to the hospital amounts to about seven or eight hundred dollars. So, Perry, who is the loser now? Who is having fun and who is having pain?"

Perry replied, "I am having pain; a lot of pain."

"There is more trouble to come. After going through a bunch of tests you will be approached by the doctors and told, 'Well, we did a lot of tests, and we're not sure what's going on with you. We need to observe you and we have a nice, fancy, glass cave hotel upstairs called the ICU for which you will pay us a few thousand dollars a day.' You are hauled to the ICU on a stretcher with tubes stuck in your arms and your nose. They also want to monitor your urinary output.

"At the I.C.U. you are greeted by more staff. Now another resident doctor approaches you with several medical students who ask you a bunch of questions. Then the doctor will come to the conclusion, 'Well . . . I need to have some consultations done to figure out what's going on with you.' A cardiologist and pulmonary specialist will examine you. They will request a Holter heart monitoring, echocardiogram, and more tests . . . for just a few thousand dollars more. When the doctor leaves, the nursing staff approaches you. Again, you are asked similar questions, your IVs are checked and you must lie still in the bed while being hooked to all of these tubes." I paused. "Perry, tell me is this pleasure or pain?"

Perry replied, "Doc, this is too much pain, I'm losing all this money."

I said, "There is still more to come on this."

He said, "What do you mean?"

I replied, "After staying in the hospital for a few days hooked up to tubes, being poked many times, going through CAT scans, and spending thousands of dollars on other tests, the doctors will come to you and tell you they figured out what's wrong. You had a mild heart attack, and they have a solution for you called pills. You will go home and take these pills two or three times a day and they will see you for a follow-up appointment.

"You think you have a solution for your problem called a pill, and pay a few hundred dollars more for your prescriptions. You come home, start taking the pills, you are anxious about your recent heart attack and you worry about your health, your wife worries about you, your children worry about you, and you start noticing that your stomach is getting upset because you have a nervous stomach all the time.

"Since the heart attack you are unable to perform sexually. You haven't realized that it is just a side effect of the medication. Your wife has been nervous-she's worried about the bills-and now she says, 'Honey, you don't love me anymore, or else you would be aroused.' Now you begin to worry about your manhood, not feeling good about yourself, and you want to see a urologist for problems with your erection and a psychiatrist for the problems of anxiety. You go see a psychiatrist, tell him you are anxious and nervous after having a heart attack, and you are not sure what's happening to your manhood. The psychiatrist says, 'I have a solution for you, Perry, in the form of antidepressants and antianxiety agents which will cost you a few hundred dollars.'"

I continued this scenario for a few more minutes. Perry pleaded, "Doc, stop! You are making me sick-this is too much pain."

I said to Perry, "Think about it . . . if you stop eating the greasy food and sacks of potato chips, what will happen?" This will help you reduce your weight. If your weight is within normal limits, your body will not wear out easily and you will have more energy so you can spend more time with your wife and children. They will be happier and you can save thousands of dollars in medical and pharmacy bills, which you can use to improve your home or take a vacation with your family members. If you're more energetic and spend more time with your wife and have no problems performing sexually, she sure will be a lot happier. Your children will be happier to see their father spending time playing basketball and other activities with them. Your boss will be happier with you because you have more energy and enthusiasm to do his work, and you won't be worried and preoccupied at work. With all the money you save, and all that new energy, you can enjoy plenty of life's pleasures."

I taught Perry to rehearse the scenario in his mind whenever he was about to go to a burger place or grab any unhealthy food. By conditioning this over and over in his mind, whenever he sees a burger or any fatty food, the scenario clicks in his brain to the extent that he feels sick to his stomach and doesn't want to eat the burger or any unhealthy food. Perry has mastered the running of his own commercial in his brain, which helps him to avoid eating greasy, unhealthy foods.

By linking it to massive amounts of pain, Perry interrupted his old behavior of eating fattening, unhealthy foods. We learned in Chapter 10, Play a New Song, that we need to replace our old patterns of behavior. In this case, he had to replace his old behavior with new behavior of eating healthy, 70 to 80 percent water-content foods, getting regular exercise, and doing deep-breathing exercises. This is further described in the Chapter 17, **Improving Energy and Health.** Thus, Perry has started eating more fruit and vegetables, drinking fresh juices, eating baked or broiled chicken and fish, cottage cheese, fresh home-baked breads, pastas, and rice. I also taught him to link pleasure to this new behavior. His wife and friends started complimenting him on how good he looks. By repeated conditioning, this new positive behavior became an automatic response for Perry to stop eating the wrong foods. He then gained pleasure from eating healthy foods.

The next step is to look into why a person eats excessive food or forms destructive habits such as excessive shopping, using drugs and alcohol excessively, or practicing promiscuous sex. Ask any person who eats excessively what they feel within themselves just before eating. Many will reply that they feel anxious, nervous, or bored, or experience some other kind of uncomfortable feeling within themselves. If we can quickly change this uncomfortable feeling of boredom, nervousness, or anxiety, it will help us to not engage in destructive habits like eating excessively. How do we do this? We learned in Chapter 6, **Conditioned Responses**, that you can link a response of happiness, calmness, peace-

WEIGHT REDUCTION

fulness, or feeling energetic to a trigger, which you can carry with you. So, whenever you feel anxious, nervous or bored before you begin eating, push the trigger and it will change your state of mind. Suddenly, you will go from boredom to feeling energetic, relaxed, happy or joyous. Then you don't have the gut feeling of being uncomfortable with a desire to eat. It is essential, in this case, to master different empowering states linked to different triggers as learned in Chapter 6, **Conditioned Responses**. By just pushing your triggers you can change your uncomfortable feeling, which will prevent you from engaging in destructive behavior. In Perry's case he pushed his trigger to feel joyous and happy whenever he wanted to change his uncomfortable gut feeling. **None of the weight loss programs in the USA have addressed this issue of managing your state of mind which drives you to eat excessively or do other destructive things such as the use of alcohol and drugs, smoking, excessive shopping, or promiscuous sex.**

The next step: Whenever you get even the slightest positive results you should link that to pleasure by rewarding yourself with a pat on your back or by any other constructive means. By repeated conditioning and practicing of these techniques you will begin doing this automatically-as automatically as you drive your car. In Perry's case, he managed to reduce his body weight to normal, get his blood pressure under control, eliminate all of the medications he was taking for hypertension, and solve the problems with his erection that resulted from the medications. He is now living a life of pleasure with his wife and family, and has a happy life. He feels great, looks younger, and has a smile on his face.

There is no failure except in no longer trying.
(Elbert Hubbard)

Chapter 13

Anger Management

This chapter is dedicated to Vietnam War veterans. I learned a lot of different techniques just by watching the veterans react to different triggers. The Vietnam War veterans have tremendous problems with anger. This anger has been very destructive to them in many areas of life. The veterans I treat tell me how anger has destroyed their lives and the lives of their families, their jobs, and many more areas of life.

These techniques can be used to get rid of many destructive emotions, destructive behavior patterns, and disempowering belief systems. In my seminars for Vietnam War veterans, I notice that whenever I talk with patients about the government, they begin to get angry and that anger escalates as we talk longer. Then they begin to curse, become loud, and sometimes pace the floor. I notice that their blood pressure begins to rise.

Any disempowering emotions will affect you physically. They can create gastrointestinal symptoms, as well as affecting your pulse rate, blood pressure, and breathing, and may also cause you to perspire. All of this plus the negative behavior associated with disempowering emotions will subsequently affect many other areas in your life. Chapters 7 and 8 explain how disempowering emotions (like anger, depression, anxiety, and fear) and disempowering meaning attached to events may affect us psychoneuroimmunologically, causing many physical problems.

The disempowering, destructive emotions can be:

1. Anger
2. Depression
3. Fear of objects, situations, surroundings; fear of failure
4. Anxiety, panic
5. Hopelessness
6. Self pity
7. Jealousy
8. Unforgiving; bitterness about past
9. Suspiciousness, paranoia; inability to trust
10. Lack of self-confidence

Some people get angry because they have a conflict with someone at work or in another area. A scenario that I bring up at the seminars is a veteran who has had a conflict with a government agency. I asked the veteran, "What happens to you when you have a conflict with the staff and you begin to get angry?" The veteran replied, "I usually start cursing, yelling, bitching about this guy, and I feel like hurting this person."
I probed further, "What happens to your stomach when you are angry?" He said, "My stomach begins churning." I further asked, "When you arrive home, because you've had a conflict at the government agency, how do you react with your spouse?" He replied, "I'm still pissed off; I'm still bitching and cursing, and I start complaining about this to my wife. My children see me being angry, cursing, yelling, and I may go off on them, too." I asked the veteran another question, "When you are still angry how do you feel in your stomach, what happens to your heart, what happens to your blood pressure, what happens to your breathing?" He answered, "My stomach is churning, my heart rate and blood pressure are up, and my breathing is very heavy as I'm pacing the floor." I said, "What do you do at that point when you are this angry?" He replied, "I take an

antacid." I told him that this provides him some relief for only a short period of time. If he continues his anger he is just starting a whole chain reaction of problems for himself and his family members.

I continued, "When you're angry, your blood pressure goes up, your pulse is rapid, and if this continues for a while you will end up seeing a doctor. If you continue to have stomach problems, you will end up going to a doctor when the antacid no longer works. The doctor sure wants to examine you, for just a few hundred dollars, and he will tell you, 'You have a problem, sir, in your stomach. We must do a test called gastroscopy to figure out what is wrong with your stomach.' He will give you an appointment to return in few days. You will have another test with fancy gastroscopes and cameras inserted into your stomach, for just a few hundred dollars more and considerable discomfort to you. After the test is over, the doctor will come to you and say, 'Well, I've found your problems! Let me show you the pictures of the holes in your stomach, called ulcers.' You look at those pictures and you feel they have figured out your problems. Now they will give you the solution for that problem, called a prescription. You'll be put on a medication called cimetidine. You take the prescription to the pharmacy and they will give you the pills, if you give them the money."

I asked the veteran, "Who is losing in this case? Who is having pleasure?" The veteran says, "I am losing and the doctors and pharmacies are getting rich." I told him that this is just the beginning of his trouble. "Think about the high blood pressure. If you continue to be angry, combined with your old habits of eating greasy foods, what will happen to you?" He replied, "I will have high blood pressure." I asked him, "Has it ever occurred to you that when you are very angry your chest starts feeling uncomfortable and your stomach starts churning?" He said, "Yes, whenever I am angry I may have chest discomfort or stomach problems." I told him that if he continues with the anger that one of these days his blood pressure may shoot up so high that his wife might have to call 9-1-1. She will become panicked and frightened as the ambulance arrives at his home with sirens wailing. He's about to begin another chain reaction of trouble, as mentioned in the previous chapter with the visit to the Emergency Room and the intensive care unit.

I let the veteran visualize the pain associated with the Emergency Room visit and hospital stay, and the medications that he would be discharged with. I let him visualize the amount of money he is losing through doctors' visits and pharmacy bills, and the side effects he may have from the pills. So, he comes home after the ICU visit with a bunch of pills, on medication for his blood pressure and an ulcer, and his anxiety and anger remains. Now he is on a medication like diazepam. He returns to work, and his employer finds out he is on a psychiatric medication for his anxiety and depression and they tell him he cannot work around machinery. They lay him off work, and when he comes home he is pissed off about losing his job and he has not yet solved any of his emotional conflicts.

I continue my narration, "Your wife still sees you angry and hostile, your children are frightened of you, and now you have the side effect from the medication so you cannot get an erection. Your wife says to you, 'First you're always angry and pissed off; we always have to live in fear. Now you've lost your job and you can't perform sexually. I have to find someone who can treat me better.' She leaves you and she takes the house and children away, sends you large bills, and asks you for alimony and child support. Now you are homeless, you have lost your family and your job, and you are on a lot of medication. Tell me who is in pain?"

He replied, "I am the one who is in massive pain because I do not manage my anger." Thus I helped the veteran link a massive amount of pain with his angry behavior. Then I helped him link a massive amount of pleasure with getting rid of his anger. I asked him, "If you are not angry when you come home and you are in a pleasant mood, how would your wife react? How would your children react?" The veteran replied, "They would treat me nicely and would like to spend time with me." I probed furher, "How do you feel when you're not angry within yourself? How is your stomach, your heart; what is happening to your pulse?" He answered, "My stomach is not churning, my heart is not beating rapidly, I'm not breathing heavily, and I'm not punching any walls."I asked him, "If you continue living without anger, how will things be between you, your wife, your family, and your employer?" He replied, "I would have a better relationship with my wife, I would not be going through a divorce, I would not have to pay legal bills, my children would want to be around me, and I would be able to keep the same job." I continued, "Would this be pleasurable?" and he replied "Yes." I taught him to condition this in his mind by rehearsing it again and again.

Next, I taught him to interrupt his old behavior pattern of anger by using techniques in Chapter 9, Emotional Record. I showed him how to interrupt the pattern by doing something unusual, something strange, funny or even ridiculous so long as it does not cause harm to himself or others. The next step is to **replace old disempowering behaviors with new empowering behaviors,** and old patterns with new patterns which will become empowering and pleasurable to him as in Chapter 10, **Play a New Song**.

In addition to this, in the seminars, I tell the veterans how to link a different meaning to the horrifying things that happened to them in the war. Remember Dr. Victor Frankl, who lived through the horror of Nazi concentration camps, and how he and others survived by linking empowering meaning to the most painful, horrifying experiences? The veterans learn to link empowering meanings to horrifying events faced in the war which haunt their lives. This is done by asking the following familiar questions:

1. What can I learn from these life experiences?
2. How can I make use of this for my family and myself?
3. How can I make use of this for humanity and the rest of the world?

Most of them answer, "We have seen enough violence in our lives and have seen how it has been destructive in our lives. We learned violence did not solve any problems. Maybe we can teach this to the children in this society who have been involved in violence."

Finally, I teach them to condition their new empowering behavior until it becomes an automatic response and link pleasure each time they have better results in relationships. People who have diligently followed through by taking daily consistent actions based upon these techniques have been able to get rid of their disempowering feelings and behavior. These techniques can be used to get rid of any disempowering emotions such as lack of self-confidence, fear, self-pity, and bitterness regarding past events. Remember, knowledge is not enough. What makes a difference is taking daily consistent actions.

Violence does not solve problems. Chronic conflicts and anger do not solve problems-they only create more problems for all of us. Conflicts are a waste of energy. Forgiveness is more powerful than anger and it creates a sense of peace and joy within us.

The strangest and most fantastic fact about negative emotions
is that people actually worship them.
(P.D. Ouspensky)

Chapter 14

Governing Values

Our value and belief system is the software of our brain. This is one of the most critical areas to understand and to knowing how it governs our behavior can create phenomenal success or disasters. It is important that our actions be synchronous with our goals and beliefs in order to create inner peace, or otherwise it will create chaos within us. Here is a list of various values which constitute our value systems:

1. Honesty
2. Competency
3. Physical fitness

4. Productivity
5. Frugality/humility

6. Serve others/contribution
7. Diligence
8. Have positive attitude
9. Organization
10. Seek truth

11. Be innovative
12. Success
13. Humor
14. Independence
15. Self-directed

16. Seek excellence
17. Generosity
18. Relationships with others
19. Willing to learn
20. Love family/children
21. Financial security
22. Self-sufficiency
23. Spirituality
24. Be a leader
25. Have integrity/loyalty
26. Intellectual growth
27. Power
28. Happiness
29. Forgiveness
30. Persistence

Values can be divided into two categories:

1. Values which are vehicles to help achieve what you are after, such as financial security, excellent relationships, etc.
2. Values which are related to states you want to achieve such as happiness, power, freedom, peace, etc.

It is important to understand our value systems and the order of their priority in our lives. Further, we must check to see that we are taking actions according to our values and goals. For example, let us take a person whose values are as follows:

1. Financial security
2. Intellectual growth
3. Relationship with others
4. Physical fitness

However, the person is spending time sleeping ten hours a day, watching TV four or five hours a day and going to a bar a couple of times a week. He or she will be in inner turmoil, because of not taking actions towards his or her goals and following the priority of his or her value system. Another example of this is a person I met who set up a goal to make $500,000 in a year. His value system is as follows:

1. Love family/children
2. Physical fitness
3. Intellectual growth
4. Financial security
5. Serve others/contribution

If this person spends fourteen hours a day trying to make money, sleeps four hours a night, spends two hours in travel to and from business, sees his wife and children for four hours a week and only talks to children one hour in a week, and has no time to read or learn new

GOVERNING VALUES

things, he will feel unfulfilled despite making money. Thus, it is important to realize the priority of the values and goals which make up our individual value systems. Next, we have to make sure our actions; values and goals are synchronous. Write down what you value the most and your goals in order of importance, then write down how and where you spent every hour in last seven days. Ask yourself a question, "Am I spending time on actions which are consistent with my goals?" If the answer is "no," change your course of action to be consistent with your value system and goals.

Values and belief systems are also critical when one gets involved in a relationship or marriage. The relationship can be with a friend, a close business relationship, or any other long-term relationship. See if your partner's value system matches yours. If both of you have similar value systems, then you both are working with similar software. If your value systems do not match, your relationship will not last long. Here is an example of the values of a couple who came to see me:

Woman	**Man**
1. Financial security	1. Love family/children
2. Independence	2. Have integrity/loyalty
3. Love	3. Financial security
4. Happiness	4. Diligence
5. Power	5. Honesty
6. Control	6. Seek excellence
7. Success	7. Intellectual growth

What would happen to this couple on a long-term basis? It would not take a rocket scientist to figure out that the relationship will not last. This couple got together initially due to a physical attraction and the common interest of travel. After their courtship they started having problems and conflicts in their relationship. There is another important aspect to values. We need to know a person's definition of each value.

The definition of the value may differ from person to person. In the above scenario, I asked the couple to write down what each value meant. These were their answers:

Woman:

1. Financially secure: To be supported by a man who will let her spend money freely, and will pay all her past-due credit card bills and taxes.
2. Independence: Going out alone and disappearing whenever she wishes.
3. Love: Sex is love.
4. Happiness: Watching TV/movies, gossiping with friends, meeting new men, traveling.
5. Power: Use of sex to control men.
6. Control: Being able to get what she wants.
7. Success: Being supported by someone; have a good personal appearance.

She had learned most of these values while growing up and seeing her parents and later her friends acting similarly.

Man:

1. Love family/children: Care for wife and children by providing for them and spending time with them.
2. Have integrity/loyalty: Be loyal to family, his work, his community, and his nation.
3. Financially secure: Have sufficient income to provide food, a nice house, insurance, cars, and funds for vacations.
4. Diligence: Constancy, zeal toward his work and home
5. Honesty: Morality, truthfulness, and fairness.
6. Seek excellence: Quality, and distinction in any task.
7. Intellectual Growth: Learn new skills, continue to get more education.

It is obvious these two people have different value systems as well as having different meanings for each value. Unless one person willingly

GOVERNING VALUES

changes his or her value system to match the other's, the relationship will fail.

I have often mentioned that we must not reinvent the wheel. It may be best to find a role model in a particular field; define their successful value system, and install it within us. Successful people have developed a value system which gives them consistent results of excelling in life. It may be worth studying the value systems of some successful people and install a similar value system in your own life. For example, if you want to be a successful businessman, it may be useful to adopt the value system of a businessman who attained the results you seek.

Some of the top priority values of successful people often include:

Persistence	Love family/children
Honesty	Seek excellence
Willing to learn	Physical fitness
Diligence	Competency
Serve others/contribution	Team player
Productivity	Organized
Intellectual growth	Innovative
Integrity/loyalty	Positive attitude

Why not adopt the value systems of successful people if you want to be successful in similar fields. One of the most important values successful people have is persistence. Take the example of Walt Disney. He had a dream of creating Disney World in Florida in the middle of an orange orchard. He went through thirteen bankruptcies before his dream came true. Did he give up? No he did not. He continued to take actions and pursue his dream of creating a magical world of entertainment.

Take another example: Thomas Alva Edison. He was one of the most prolific inventors of the nineteenth century. He was trying to invent the incandescent lamp. He began work on an electric lamp and sought a material that could be electrically heated to incandescence in a vacuum. At first he used platinum wire in glass bulbs at ten volts. Edison conducted an extensive search for a filament material to replace platinum until, on October 21, 1879, he demonstrated a lamp with carbonized cotton thread that glowed for forty hours. It took him several hundred attempts to succeed. He also persisted in taking actions to reach his goal. He said, "I am not discouraged, because every wrong attempt discarded is a step ahead."

Another example is the Lexus car. The company set a goal of capturing the luxury car market which was dominated by Mercedes Benz, BMW, and Porsche. Most Americans who purchased luxury cars believed that nobody could take the place of these automobiles. But Lexus set a goal of creating the best luxury automobile and succeeded in reaching that goal by the constant pursuit of perfection. They were reported by Consumer Reports to have the best luxury car for several years in a row after their introduction. The Lexus motto is, "Relentless pursuit of perfection."

Another example is General Colin Powell. He grew up in South Bronx and succeeded despite many adversities.

Abraham Lincoln is another interesting example. **The values of courage, perseverance and persistence are clearly illustrated in the life story of Abraham Lincoln:i**

Experience	Age
Failed in business	22
Ran for legislature-defeated	23
Again failed in business	24
Elected to legislature	25
Sweetheart died	26
Had a nervous breakdown	27

GOVERNING VALUES

Defeated for speaker	29
Defeated for elector	31
Defeated for congress	34
Elected for congress	37
Defeated for congress	39
Defeated for the senate	46
Defeated for vice president	47
Defeated for the senate	49
Elected president of the United States	51

If you continue to take actions towards your goal, you will ultimately reach it. Most of the time we quit because of a conditioned response installed in us by someone else (or ourselves) that "this is impossible." Mahatma Gandhi set up a goal of getting the British out of India. If he would have come to you or me with this idea we would have laughed at him and said something like, "You're crazy, this is impossible. How can you get the British out of India by non-violent means when the British rule most of the world?" Did Mahatma Gandhi succeed at his goal? He achieved that goal by taking persistent actions for many years.

Another important value is integrity. One of the definitions of integrity in the Oxford dictionary is "the character of uncorrupted virtue, especially in relation to truth and fair dealing, sincerity." Until you are true to yourself and true to others, you will have tremendous difficulties trying to succeed. People of true integrity have the same behavior during good times or bad times or when dealing with any adversaries. They remain caring and true friends or partners even in difficult times. I have had the personal experience of meeting people who are nice when they feel they can have financial gains in business or relationships. When they realized there might not be any financial gain, they disappeared.

It is also important to see if our value systems are in tune with nature, or the universe. My biggest role model when adopting a value system comes from nature. Nature teaches us not to be selfish and to share resources. Nature teaches us to contribute to each other. Nature is constantly sharing its resources of air, water, food and all other material things. Imagine what would happen if nature said, "Do not use my air and water for two weeks. It is my water, my air, and my Earth which is creating these resources." Nature operates by keeping everything working in harmony with the least effort. Nature is constantly recirculating all the resources of air, water, and food. Nature wants us to live in harmony on this planet, as we are all part of it.

Most of the problems of mankind are created by man, and the solutions to those problems are within all of us. This book provides a key to find those solutions within yourself. **Check to see if your value system is in tune with nature. This will help us all live in harmony and peace.** Let us look at some of the values of nature:

1. Contribute to each other
2. Love each other and family
3. Infinite organization of events
4. Self-sufficiency
5. Forgiveness

Build your value system based on the values of successful people. Do not reinvent the wheel. Build a value system which is empowering to you, your family, your neighbors, and humanity. It will give you ultimate joy and the sense of success.

> *Don't be afraid to take a big step if one is indicated.*
> *You can't cross a chasm in two small jumps.*
> (David Lloyd George)

---

i Bits & Pieces, the Magazine that Motivates the World. Vol. R/No. 29. Fairfield, NJ: The Economic Press, 1997.

Chapter 15

Belief: Empowering or Disempowering

What is belief? One of the meanings of belief in the Oxford dictionary is "mental acceptance of a proposition, statement or fact as true on the ground of authority or evidence; assent of mind to a statement; a fact on evidence of consciousness.[1]

What is a belief system? Beliefs are opinions that you have formed (often unconsciously), which are based upon your past experiences or teachings from others. You will feel certain about your belief systems, whether they are healthy and good for you or not, because you have accumulated "evidence" to support them. Belief systems are guidelines you adopt or create about how life, business, relationships, etc. can be conducted.

One example is the belief system I have which is: Having a better education will create a better future for myself and my family. Where did I get this belief system? It came from my parents who taught me that education would get me a better job and help me create a better future for my family and myself. While growing up I was also exposed to cousins who attended various colleges, and their experiences reinforced my belief that having a better education helps to create a better future. So, I had gathered enough evidence to support my belief system that having a good education could create a successful future.

Other belief systems can be destructive, such as in the case of children who grow up in ghetto areas around drug dealers, selling drugs and carrying guns. They develop a belief system that doing the drugs, carrying guns and using violence is just a way of life. These children have gathered enough evidence while growing up to support this belief system.

We need to look into our belief systems and see which ones are empowering and which ones are disempowering.

Beliefs are created as conditioned responses from our experiences and environment, and they make us respond automatically based upon those conditioned responses. These experiences may come from teachers, parents, friends, acquaintances, movies, TV, personal experiences, or the many thousands of stimuli to which we are exposed daily. Many Americans believed a few years ago that "Russia is an evil empire." Now many of us realize that they are people like you and me with similar feelings, needs, and fears. I have made some Russian friends, and they are as human and normal as my friends in the USA and other countries. Yet just a few years ago I was made to believe that Russia was an evil empire by constant exposure to this concept in the news and from the mouths of biased political leaders.

Let me take another example of someone I met in the past who was a patient in an alcohol and drug rehab program. She believed everyone she knew did cocaine. She had gathered enough evidence for this belief by being around many people who used cocaine. The truth of matter is that more than 50 percent of the people in the state of Missouri do not use cocaine, yet this person believed that everyone used it. Have you known people who believe that everyone drinks alcohol and gets drunk occasionally, and that you cannot have a party unless you have booze? I wonder how they acquired this belief system? There are a substantial percentage of people who do not drink and yet they still have excellent parties. Ask an alcoholic who has sobered up, and he will tell you he started finding these people when

BELIEF: EMPOWERING OR DISEMPOWERING

he became sober and now has fun in his life, attends parties, and enjoys football games-all without drinking.

Beliefs can be empowering or disempowering. Let us look at just a few of them. Of course, a complete list of all possible beliefs is beyond the scope of this book, but this should get you thinking about some of your own.

Empowering Beliefs	Disempowering Beliefs
People generally care for each other.	People are always manipulative.
Honesty leads me to have a fearless life.	Almost everyone is dishonest.
Hard work and smart actions lead to success.	Manipulation and bribery will lead to success.
Persistence will lead to success.	I have tried many times without success so I will never succeed.
Past experiences teach me what doesn't work.	Past experiences have taught me I will fail.
Each rejection teaches me why I have been failing. I learn from it to change my approach.	I have been rejected many times; therefore I will be rejected again. I am afraid of rejection.
With each rejection I get closer to success.	With each rejection I am convinced I am bound to fail.
The ability to communicate is within me.	People don't treat me well is because of my accent.

Find out your own empowering and disempowering beliefs. Make a list of them on paper and get rid of the disempowering beliefs by techniques shown below and in previous chapters. Then work on strengthening your empowering beliefs. Remember to not reinvent the wheel. Let us use the same process which helped us in the past to change some of our belief system and helped James to quit smoking. We went, for example from the belief that "smoking is pleasurable" to the belief that "smoking is painful and causes death." Let us not wait till we come close to as painful a situation as death to change our disempowering belief systems.

1. **Set up a goal of getting rid of disempowering beliefs.** Have a precise goal to be free of your disempowering beliefs.

2. **Associate massive pain to continuing disempowering beliefs.** Visualize how these disempowering beliefs will affect your life: physically, financially, in relationships, spiritually, and any other way you can imagine, over a period of days, weeks, or months. Visualize where you will be in a year, in five years, in ten years, and in twenty years if you continue your disempowering beliefs. This will help you create massive pain. Remember that you are creating your own advertising commercial to link massive pain to disempowering beliefs, which will make your brain run away from the painful beliefs.

3. **Associate massive pleasure to getting rid of disempowering beliefs**. Visualize how losing your disempowering beliefs will affect your life physically, financially, in relationships, spiritually, etc., over a period of days, weeks, months, and years. Associate pleasure to every aspect of life when you get rid of the disempowering beliefs. Visualize in detail the pleasurable experiences you will have because you are free of the disempowering beliefs.

4. **Interrupt your old belief system by scratching your old record as you learned in Chapter 9, Emotional Record.**

5. **Replace your old beliefs with new empowering beliefs as you learned in Chapter 10, Play a New Song.** Give a new meaning to the old belief by repetition. For example, "Failure is in my head;

BELIEF: EMPOWERING OR DISEMPOWERING

each attempt is a step toward success," or, "Each rejection (for example in sales) teaches me what does not work and helps me find new ways of being accepted or successful." Condition your mind by repetition. Remember you can associate any meaning to any event. Associate an empowering meaning to each attempt, which will help you improve your focus, concentration, and energy level.

6. **Push your trigger/anchor to enter empowering states of feeling energetic, calm, peaceful, or invincible.** By repeating this process you can condition your mind to react as automatically as it does when you are driving your car. Remember that driving a car is much more complex than your present task.

People who have succeeded the most have gone through more failures and rejections than the average person, but they label failures and rejections differently. They call them steps towards success. Remember the example of Thomas Edison. He attempted hundreds of times before succeeding. He said, "I am not discouraged because every attempt discarded is a step ahead." Another example of this is when I ask people in a seminar, "Can you ride a bicycle?" They say "yes," and then I ask them, "Did you fall while learning to ride a bicycle?" They look at me and say, "Of course; yes." So then I ask them, "Did you stop yourself from trying to learn to ride after you had fallen a few times?" They look at me as if I am asking a bizarre question and answer, "No, I kept trying until I learned." I ask them then, "So why would you stop yourself from trying to achieve a goal now, even if you fall a few times?"

You may define success in such a way that it makes it easy for you to feel successful. For example, instead of calling each unsuccessful attempt a failure, you may call it a success as you have learned something from each attempt. If you make it difficult on yourself to feel successful, you will end up in a disempowering state. If you make it easy to feel successful, it will put you in an empowering state, which will create more enthusiasm to take further action.

One person may believe success can only be achieved after the first or second try. A second person may see success as achieving a goal after many trials and learning from each attempt what does not work and what might work. This person perceives that as long as he is learning something from his attempts he is successful. In the first case the person has set up a meaning or belief which will make him prone to entering a disempowering state and feeling a failure. The second example is a person who has attached a meaning or belief that will put him in an empowering state after each attempt and will ultimately lead to success. Now let us compare this to people who have already succeeded. Of course we do not want to reinvent the wheel so we will examine the belief systems employed by successful people.

Consider Walt Disney who had thirteen bankruptcies, or Colonel Sanders who finally sold his chicken recipe after more than a thousand attempts, or the man who invented Kleenex and sold the idea only after multiple attempts. There are hundreds of such examples. Albert Einstein once said, "I think and think for years and years. Ninety-nine times, the conclusion is false. The hundredth time I am right." So what can we learn from these people? Success may mean achieving a goal after many trials and learning from each attempt what works and what does not. My personal definition or belief about being successful is, "If I have worked hard and given more than 100 percent to each attempt, I will have learned something and I will have succeeded." Make sure that every action you take or belief you have falls into the category of **Actions for Success or Actions for Improvement** as described in Chapter 3.

Here are some of my old belief systems:
1. Public speaking is not for me.

BELIEF: EMPOWERING OR DISEMPOWERING

2. Those who have become businessmen in life were born businessmen from the start.
3. Salesmen are born, not made. One cannot become a salesman later in life.

After realizing that all of these beliefs were false, I was able to break the old belief system and create new empowering belief systems. I find pleasure and excitement in public speaking now. In addition, I have built a business and have learned how to sell.

Many times we respond to rejection, failure, and fear based upon belief systems imposed upon us knowingly or unknowingly by our environment, including our parents, schools, peers, friends, movies, TV, news media, co-workers, and many other circumstances in our environment. Most of the time when we react to rejection, failure, or fear, we are responding based upon past conditioned responses, created in us from past experiences.

A good example of this is when a man is challenged in a bar. Now, he may have been taught that he can be a macho man by getting into a fight; however, for a successful life he needs to create a new empowering belief system from within himself, which will fall into the categories of Actions for Success or Actions for Improvement. If someone curses at him, his old conditioned response or belief system may tell him to curse the person back or get angry and initiate a fight. What would happen in this case? Both people would get hurt either physically or emotionally, or both. Just imagine how they would both feel after the fight. They would feel angry and irritable or have other uncomfortable feelings within themselves. They may even get physically hurt and end up with serious injuries. This kind of response falls into **Actions for Disaster or Actions that are Crazy.** This man's new conditioned belief or response may be, "I do not have to accept someone's cursing or verbal abuse. I do not have to respond in a yo-yo fashion to an old conditioned response.

I can remain calm and peaceful." When the other person realizes their cursing, yelling, and screaming have not affected him even slightly, they will feel powerless because they were unable to control the situation and elicit anger from the man. As you can see, it is important to create an empowering belief or a response from within yourself that is not dependent on outside stimuli.

A friend of mine who understood this concept had gone to a Thai restaurant with his ex-wife from whom he had been recently divorced. While in the restaurant, the ex-wife started blaming my friend for all the misery and problems she was experiencing. She continued blaming him, and when he did not respond with his usual past defensive behavior, she started cursing him and using a lot of profanity. On their way back home she continued to curse, yell, scream, and make hideously insulting remarks just to make him angry and lose control. He remained perfectly calm and peaceful. When they reached home, he told her to leave-to return to her apartment-and take all the cursing with her. There wasn't the slightest distress in his behavior. She was expecting him to react with anger and defend himself. The next day she called him several times and left several messages that she was very sorry for her behavior.

Learn to create power within yourself, instead of responding to outside stimuli, like a yo-yo to a conditioned disempowering response. The following examples will clarify this concept.

Stimulus from Environment	**Conditioned Responses**
1. Someone curses you.	You may curse back or get angry.
2. Someone makes a pleasant comment.	You feel pleased.
3. Someone challenges you in a bar.	You fight to prove you're strong, manly.
4. You see ads for brand-name items.	Feel worthy wearing brand-name clothes.
5. TGIF syndrome prevails.	You feel it is time to party.

BELIEF: EMPOWERING OR DISEMPOWERING

When people have a belief system which makes them feel worthy only if they have brand-name clothes, titles, or certain automobiles, they are prisoners of past conditioned responses. If you have this problem and learn to break your past disempowering conditioned beliefs and strengthen your new empowering beliefs, you can create phenomenal results in your life. Remember our earlier example of Mahatma Gandhi. If he had allowed himself to have the disempowering belief that his goal of getting the British to leave India was impossible, he never would have succeeded. How many times do we stop ourselves by saying, "This is impossible"? I used to do it myself, and I have realized that once you destroy your past disempowering belief, make a decision to reach a goal, and take daily consistent actions, you can reach almost any goal.

The following diagram will illustrate how we usually respond with the yo-yo effect to past conditioned responses/conditioned beliefs. **Learn to break past disempowering conditioned beliefs and strengthen empowering beliefs, then you can create phenomenal results in life.**

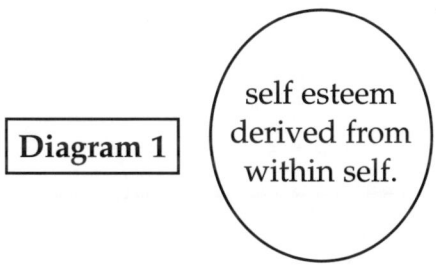

Diagram 2

The second diagram shows we are prisoners of conditioned responses.

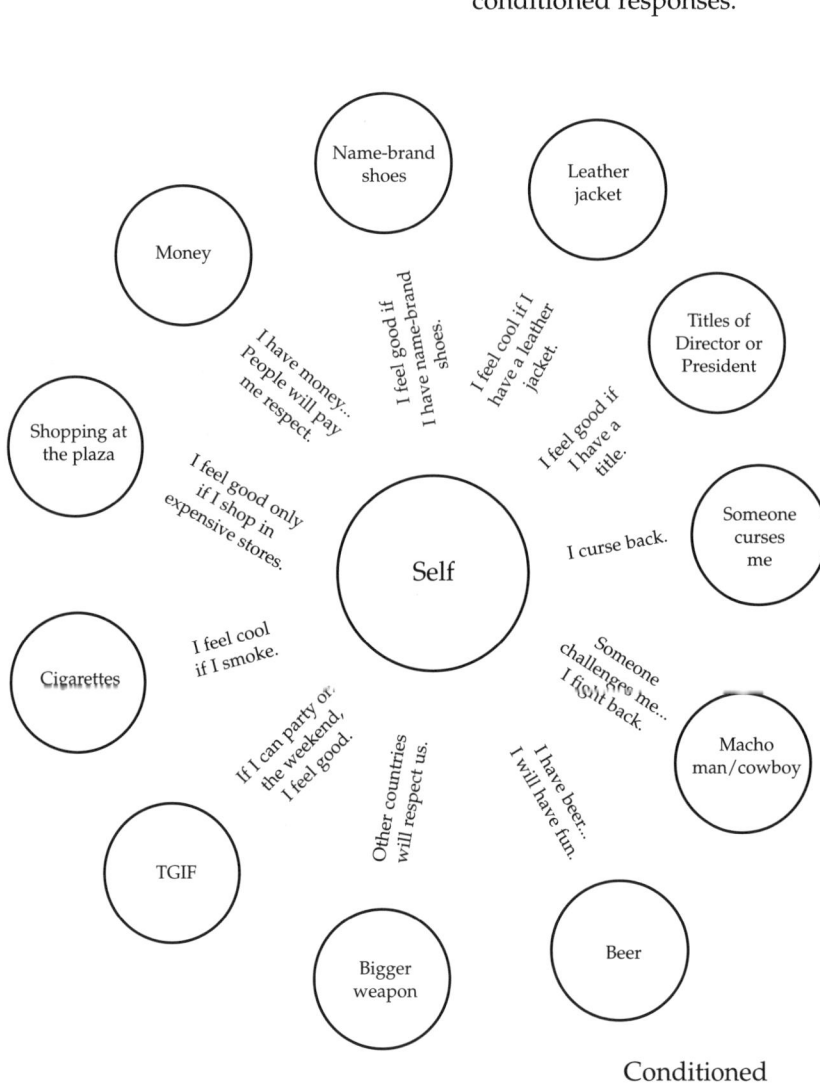

Conditioned responses

Your value and belief systems may make you or break you.

BELIEF: EMPOWERING OR DISEMPOWERING

Inventors and Belief System

Many times my audiences ask me how to invent different ideas and products. We need to realize that most of us are locked into belief systems or perceptions instilled in us by millions of people. We believe that articles, objects, or products can be created and projects can be done in only certain ways. A U.S. government official said during the last century, "Man has invented everything he can invent, there can be no more invention." What a myth that was. We have been inventing literally thousands of items each year. To invent any new ideas, one must negate the belief system instilled in them by millions of others. One has to look at things from outside with the intention that they can be manifested in different ways than most people believe. The invention starts in an inventor's head by breaking through this belief system. Every object you are seeing around you was first created in someone's head. Once you understand the process it becomes easy to invent new ideas.

Let me give you a few examples. If the Wright brothers would have walked up to people and announced, "We are going to fly in these pieces of wood strapped together with an engine attached to them, most people would have laughed at them, saying, Are you drunk or crazy? You must be losing your mind." Most people were stuck in the belief system or perception that man could not make an object which is heavier than air fly up in the air. Of course, all you have to do now is look at a jumbo jet, which is the size of a football field. It will make you realize how wrong that limited belief system was. Let me give you an another example.

If Thomas Edison would have approached people and told them (before they had ever seen an electric bulb), that he was going to make a piece of wire glow in the dark and that they would no longer need the oil lamps, they would have laughed at him, saying, "Are you crazy? You cannot make a piece of wire glow in the dark and light the whole room." Did he succeed? He did. Why? Because he broke through the limitations of the belief system that his society had instilled in him. The ability to create anything is within all of us. What stops us are our own locked-in perceptions and belief systems. Tap into this ability.

> *Sooner or later every one of us breathes an atom of air*
> *that has been breathed before by anyone you can think of*
> *who has lived before us - Michelangelo or*
> *George Washington or Moses.*
> (Jacob Bronowski)

---

[1] Oxford English Dictionary, Compact Edition. 25th ed. Oxford: Oxford University Press, 1986.

Chapter 16

Opportunities to Grow

In the first chapter we learned not to reinvent the wheel. Let us look at how successful people have dealt with what we call a problem. Did these following people face problems?

1. As a young lawyer, Mahatma Gandhi was called the equivalent of a "nigger" and thrown out of a train in South Africa.
2. The mother who formed Mothers Against Drunk Driving was faced with the death of her daughter caused by a drunk driver.
3. Thomas Edison made several hundred attempts before he created the lightbulb.
4. Colonel Sanders faced retirement with less than $100 a month income and did not have a substantial education.
5. Lee Iacocca was fired from Ford at middle age.
6. Martin Luther King, Jr. faced discrimination all his life as an African-American.

Many other successful people have faced numerous problems. How did they deal with them? Did they start getting anxious, depressed, hopeless, and angry? Did they curse, kick chairs, take a drink or do drugs? Did they feel that things would never change and say, "I cannot change this," and lose their concentration? Let us find the Pentium chip or a recipe from these people who successfully faced massive problems. They were people just like you and me, before they became famous and changed the world.

Let us look at how most people react to problems when faced with them. What are our usual reactions? When faced with problems we feel:

1. Frustrated
2. Angry
3. Anxious, nervous
4. Depressed, sad
5. Overwhelmed
6. Hopeless
7. Will never resolve this
8. Why me? Poor me?

Let us look as what happens when we get into these states. When we feel frustrated, angry, depressed, sad, overwhelmed, or any of the emotions mentioned above, **our ability to deal with problems decreases**. In fact, our ability to deal with problems is reduced tremendously, as we cannot concentrate on looking for solutions. **We enter a disempowering state, which is due to these emotions, and this will make it much more difficult to solve these problems**. What outcome do we seek when we are faced with these problems? The outcome we want is to find solutions to these problems and reach our goals. If we become frustrated, angry, irritable, depressed, sad, or hopeless, our ability to deal with problems or find solutions **decreases,** because our mind does not focus or cannot concentrate on how to look for solutions. Some people use alcohol or take drugs when faced with problems. Both alcohol and drugs will compound and magnify any problem.

What did Thomas Edison do when he failed hundreds of times while trying to create a lightbulb? Did he enter a disempowering state? No. The first thing he did was to give a different meaning to each trial, an empowering meaning. As we quoted in Chapter 15, he said, "I am not discouraged because every attempt discarded is a step ahead." Thus he gave an empowering meaning to each problem, which helped

OPPORTUNITIES TO GROW

to keep him in an empowering state of mind. When he was in this empowering state, he could concentrate better, and had more energy to keep looking for solutions. Ultimately, when he succeeded, Edison said, "Success was 1 percent inspiration and 99 percent perspiration!"

Can you do this? Yes, you can. We learned in an earlier chapter that we can link any meaning to any event. If we define the problem differently and link it to an empowering meaning, it will get us into an empowering state. **We can define every problem as a seed of opportunity and growth. Every failed attempt teaches us what does not work and that we should look for other ways to reach our goal.** This will get us into an empowering state.

What are empowering states?
1. Happy, excited
2. Enthused
3. Calm, peaceful
4. Energetic
5. Invincible, powerful

Yes, you can link to an empowering meaning when faced with problems. You can also call them adventures. We can use what we learned earlier in Chapter 7, **Empowering Meaning to Any Event**, which was how to link the meaning of your choice to any event. You can also get into an energetic and excited state when faced with problems by pushing your triggers as you learned in Chapter 6, **Conditioned Responses.** You are in an excited state when you are faced with adventure and ready to grow. What if Thomas Edison had given up? What would have happened? Think about what will happen if you give up on your goals when you are faced with problems.

Did the Wright brothers have problems when they were inventing the airplane and trying to get it off the ground? Yes, they had many problems. If they had given up, we would not be flying from one continent to another in a few hours. **Problems are part of life for everyone**. Both the president of the United States and Saddam Hussein have numerous problems. What makes people successful is how they tackle these problems. I have never seen any person in my whole life who has not faced any problems. Have you? Problems are going to come, no matter who you are. **The difference in successful people is how they tackle problems without getting into a disempowering state. Successful people have far more problems than most other people do**.

Every problem that you face is an opportunity in disguise. As we said earlier, **every problem is a seed of opportunity and growth**. The problems in Colonel Sander's life helped him to grow, start Kentucky Fried Chicken and become wealthy. The problems in Lee Iacocca's life helped him to run Chrysler, turn it around into a success, and become a famous role model for millions. The problems in Martin Luther King Jr.'s life and Mahatma Gandhi's lives helped them to create massive changes in the societies in which they lived and the world. Without those problems, they would not have achieved what they did in their lives. Thus every problem is an opportunity for us to grow, expand, and broaden our horizons.

Usually all of us live within a comfort zone. My comfort zone may be just being able to pay my bills and manage my bank balance based upon my salary. If somebody crashes into my car and runs off, and I have to get the car fixed, which was not part of my tight budget, I suddenly have a problem because I have an extra financial burden. If I become overwhelmed, frustrated, and angry, what is going to happen? I will have difficulty finding a solution to this problem, and I will feel even more overwhelmed. On the other hand if I remain calm (empowering state), I will be more focused and able to find a solution to this problem. Every time we are faced with a problem and learn to solve it, we expand our horizons and thus expand our comfort zones. We grow

OPPORTUNITIES TO GROW

in many different directions with each problem we face. This is helping us meet our human requirement of growth, as mentioned in Chapter 3, **Actions for Success**. Instead of becoming frustrated when we are faced with problems, we can stay calm and thus we will be better equipped to deal with and find solutions to these problems.

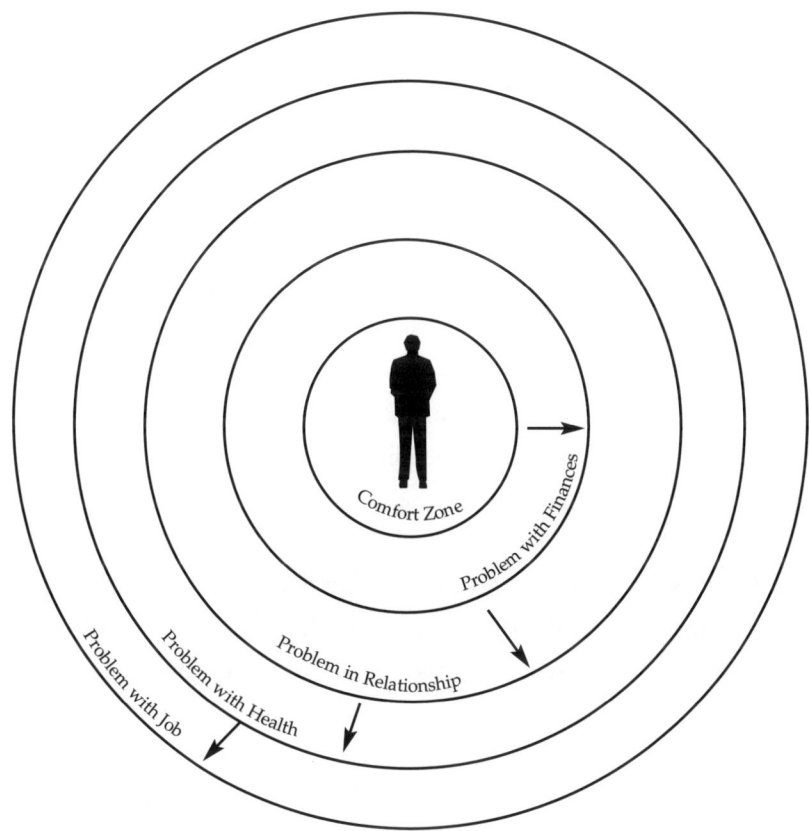

The above diagram will help you to understand how facing a problem and solving it will help you expand your horizons of continued growth.

Just look at your own life. You have been faced with many problems in the past that taught you how to deal with situations and grow.

You have learned many things by dealing with those problems and finding answers to them. Let me give you an example of what happens to some people who avoid dealing with problems, who feel that problems should not occur, and the end result of this.

I have worked in VA hospitals with a domicillary. The patients who live at the domicillary have housing and a support system. When they enter the domicillary they possess several skills which have enabled them to face many difficulties; however, when they start living at the domicillary, everything is done for them and they do not have to face as many problems. They are provided food and recreational activities and they are told what to do, when and where they can go for therapy, etc. As they stay at the domicillary longer and longer, their ability to deal with problems decreases to the point that they cannot face even simple tasks, like going into a store to buy some items, or going to a job interview. This happens because their comfort zone keeps shrinking and because they lose the skills of dealing with common life problems so they start perceiving simple tasks as stressful.

Another example of this is when people are moved from working people's neighborhoods to welfare housing. Many who start living in the welfare housing will not have role models to show them how to cope with and solve problems.

Let us take the example of Mother Teresa. She was faced with the problem of seeing people suffering from hunger and disease. What did she do? She associated massive amounts of pain with seeing this problem, and associated pleasure with taking care of those who suffer from hunger and disease. This drove her to take monumental actions to help these people. Did she make a difference in this world and help thousands? Yes she did. What made her take action was associating massive pain with the problem of hunger and suffering and pleasure with solving the problem. We have learned what propels behavior is avoiding pain or gaining

OPPORTUNITIES TO GROW

pleasure. We learned in Chapter 4, **The Two Masters,** how to associate pain and pleasure with any event. **You can associate a massive amount of pain with not solving problems and a massive amount of pleasure with solving problems. Associate a massive amount of pain with feeling frustrated, angry and irritable, or with any disempowering state as listed above, and associate pleasure with the empowering states.**

Your problems may be with a relationship, health, finances, or in some other area of life. If you start feeling angry, sad, depressed, or overwhelmed, it is just going to create more pain in your life. On the other hand, if you learn to solve these so-called problems, you will be growing, expanding, and having the pleasure of conquering new horizons. The next thing to do is focus attention on how you are going to solve the problems instead of dwelling on the problem itself. Look for solutions, look for what you can do to find solutions. If you don't know how to find solutions, find a role model as we have shown in the first two chapters of this book. Spend time looking for solutions to these problems, instead of just dwelling on them.

Take action to solve problems and keep taking action as shown in Chapter 2, **Hit the Bull's-Eye Every Time.** Find out if the actions you are taking are moving you toward a solution. Discard the actions that are taking you away from solving problems. If your actions are taking you away from solving the problems, change direction. The easiest way to find solutions to problems is to find a recipe for them. There are people on this planet who have faced similar problems and have found ways to solve them. Somebody on this planet has gone through similar problems and mastered the solutions to those problems. Instead of reinventing the wheel, find a set of wheels or a recipe that somebody has used to solve those problems. Take mammoth actions to solve your problems. If you follow a recipe exactly on how to solve problems you will have similar results. **As I say, there are no new problems to mankind. There is someone somewhere who has faced** similar problems and has mastered a solution to them. Go find the recipe, follow it, and you will have the same results as the other person. Whenever you are facing problems, ask yourself the following questions:

1. What can I learn from this?
2. What is it that nature is trying to teach me from these problems?
3. How can I benefit from this problem?
4. How can other fellow human beings benefit from this?
5. How can this problem be beneficial to planet earth, nature and humanity?
6. How can I have ultimate fulfillment from this?

If you ask these questions, you will start finding answers. It will change how you approach problems. If you master these skills, you will realize that whenever you are faced with any problem (which I call an opportunity to grow), you will become thrilled and will look at it as an opportunity to grow and expand your life instead of feeling overwhelmed, nervous, anxious, or hopeless. Why not see problems as an adventure to help you grow in this life and expand your horizons, as well as use it to benefit mankind?

Now let us look at some people who faced problems. For example, Candy Lightner's daughter was killed by a drunk driver and she started Mothers Against Drunk Driving. What did she do? She gave a different meaning to this tragedy. She asked similar questions to those above and came up with excellent answers, which empowered her. The specific questions were, "How can I make use of this for myself and how can I help humanity?" What did she do? She started an organization to make people aware of what drunk driving does to people and how people are killed because of it. She focused on her seventh human requirement, "Service to humanity." Meeting your seventh human requirement as you learned in Chapter 3, Actions for Success, will create ultimate joy, ultimate fulfillment. The great leaders of the

OPPORTUNITIES TO GROW

world like Mahatma Gandhi, Martin Luther King, Jr., and Mother Teresa focused on "Service to humanity." Did Candy Lightner make a difference in the world? Yes, she did. **You can make a difference within yourself and in the lives of others. The ability to do it is within you–tap into it! Problems in life help us grow and seek new opportunities.**

Victory belongs to the most persevering.
(Napolean)

Chapter 17

Improving Energy and Health

If you want to succeed in all areas of life, the most critical area to understand is how and to have enhanced health and a higher energy level. You may set up goals to make money, have better relationships, travel all over the world, enjoy life, but if your health is not great and if you do not have plenty of energy, you will not be able to enjoy your wealth and relationships, and have all the fun you want. I personally have been able to work fourteen hours a day, Monday through Sunday, 365 days a year and enjoy life, just by making some simple lifestyle changes and improving my health.

The most important source of energy is oxygen, which is around us all the time. I asked the participants of my seminar, "If I'm deprived of food, how long will I live?" The audience answered, "Approximately two weeks." Then I asked, "If you deprive me of water, how long will I survive?" The audience replied, "Four to five days." Then I asked, "If you deprive me of oxygen, how long will I survive?" The audience replied, "Maybe five to ten minutes." So what is the most important ingredient of energy? It is oxygen, which is available in abundance all around us.

How does each cell in the human body function? If I want to walk around, my muscles have to function. They need energy and all this happens at a cellular level. If I want to just think, it happens in the brain at a cellular level. If I want to look at someone, it still happens at a cellular level in my eyes and occipital cortex. If I want to have sex, arousal happens on a cellular level. If you want to fight or curse, the impetus happens on a cellular level. So, literally any activity you want to do happens on a cellular level. Each cell needs oxygen and a few calories to create energy and function. Our bodies are like a car engine, except our fuel, causing combustion and creating energy, is oxygen/air and the calories consumed in the food we eat.

How do you get oxygen into the body? We breathe in oxygen from the environment around us into our lungs. If you want to provide more energy to every cell in your body you must breathe in deeply. Oxygen in the air gets exchanged in the lungs and enters the blood circulation. If you want to move your finger, the oxygen needed to do this has to be transported from the lungs to the tip of your finger. If you want to look at someone, you need oxygen to be transported from your lungs to your eyes and to part of your brain. If you want to cook or do any physical activity, oxygen needs to be carried from the lungs to the specific muscles.

Now imagine if you were to choke me. What would happen? I would be dead in five to ten minutes, but before I died cellular damage would occur due to the lack of oxygen. Imagine cutting off the circulation to your arm. The cells in your arm would deteriorate before they died. Thus, if there is poor oxygen transportation from the lungs to every part of your body and every cell in your body it will cause cellular damage.

Your cardiovascular system is nothing but a mega-pipeline with the heart as its pump. If we take all the blood vessels in the human body and stretch them end-to-end they will be approximately sixty thousand miles in length. Imagine a garden hose that is carrying water from one end to the other. If the inside of the garden hose gets clogged, the water will not flow properly. Imagine if this were to happen inside your blood vessels. The blood vessels in your forearms or hands are big enough to see with the naked eye. The blood vessels in the tips of your fingers are extremely tiny and cannot be seen with the naked eye.

IMPROVING ENERGY AND HEALTH

I have asked audiences many times in seminars to take a piece of sausage, cut it up into small pieces, put it on a plate, and heat it in a microwave oven. Then, take the plate and pour it on the side of a cold kitchen sink. What do they see? Most people have replied that they saw a lot of thick, semi-solid grease. Now imagine putting this grease into your blood vessels! It wouldn't take much grease to occlude tiny blood vessels in the tips of your fingers, in your brain or any part of your body. One does not need too much grease to occlude the tiniest blood vessels. If you occlude the blood vessels it will cause cellular damage to the areas the blood vessels are supplying.

I often ask another question, "Do you drive an automobile?" Most reply "yes." Then I asked one of the participants, "Would you put a can of oil in the gas tank of your car?" The man always replies, "No, sir." When I ask, "Why not?" he replies, "The car would sputter and the engine would die." I then ask the audience, "Then why would you do such a thing to your own body?" Generally they reply that they never thought about it this way before. If you occlude the blood vessels with the grease from hamburgers, french fries, sausages, and other high fat foods your body will start to sputter and gradually slow down, similar to the car sputtering if you put a can of oil in its gas tank.

As I showed earlier the oxygen needs to be transported quickly from the lungs to every cell in the body where required. This transportation occurs through the red blood cells, which are carried through the blood, which in turn is carried through the blood vessels. Blood has two main constituents. They are the cells or corpuscles (red blood cells, white blood cells and platelets) and plasma. Blood cells are carried through plasma, which is approximately 90 percent water. If you keep your blood fluid, the red blood cells which carry oxygen will be transported rapidly from the lungs to the end tissues and provide oxygen to each cell. If the blood circulates faster, it will improve oxygenation to each cell thus providing more energy, and improving the life of each cell. How do you manage that?

If you do regular exercise at least four to five times a week for twenty to thirty minutes it will improve your circulation. I suggest exercise independent of barriers like having the company of a friend, having nice weather to travel to a gymnasium, or being worried about personal appearance while going to a health club. Most of us have been taught exercise in school. If you have equipment at home go ahead and use it on an everyday basis. Most of us can get enough exercise without using any equipment. One can have a daily routine of stretching different muscles/joints, warm-up exercises, push-ups, sit-ups, and couple of miles of walking or jogging. **The trick is to exercise almost every day.**

When one does regular exercise it stimulates the circulation of blood and thus the circulation of red blood cells, from the lungs to the tissue cells and back to the lungs. If your blood moves faster, you will have oxygen moving faster from your lungs to the various cells in your body. As we said earlier the source of energy is oxygen and nutrients. If each cell in the body gets plenty of oxygen and nutrients this will improve your energy level and longevity. By doing regular exercise you have the multiple benefits of improving blood flow to your brain, heart, muscles, bones, joints, and every other cell in your body. This will improve the functioning capacity and vitality of every cell in your body. It doesn't cost you anything, and it can be done without putting any pills into your body. It is similar to the fuel injectors of a new car. If the fuel injectors are clogged and if there is not enough fuel going into your car it won't have enough power. In addition, exercise can decrease anxiety and improve your ability to deal with stress.

For best results, combine regular physical exercise with deep breathing exercises. I like to stress the importance of deep breathing. Yoga, Tai-chi and most other exercise practices stress the importance of deep diaphragmatic breathing every day. Sit in a quiet place in a comfortable position. Breathe in deeply, then hold your breath, and then slowly breathe out. **Do this in a ratio of 1:4:2.** This simply means if you

IMPROVING ENERGY AND HEALTH

breathe in for two seconds hold the breath for eight seconds and breathe out for four seconds. **Essentially this involves holding your breath and breathing out longer than breathing in**. Repeat this for four to five minutes or as tolerable at the beginning. Focus on your breath while doing so. Doing this simple exercise improves the oxygen exchange in your lungs as you hold the breath longer in your lungs. When you exhale longer you are helping to eliminate waste products in your body. It will also improve lymphatic circulation. The lymphatic vessels drain the waste products of dead tissue as well as work with the immune system. The lymphatic system does not have a pump like the heart in the cardiovascular system. Most major lymph vessels run along the inside of the chest wall. Deep breathing exercises create a negative suction pressure in the chest cavity and therefore a suctioning effect on the lymph vessels. This in turn improves lymph circulation. Deep breathing exercises have the advantage of improving both oxygenation and the immune system. Do the deep breathing exercises two to three times a day, which will barely take ten to fifteen minutes of time. There are many variations of deep breathing exercises. Yoga, martial arts, Ayurveda and many other disciplines teach deep breathing exercises. I initially learned the deep breathing exercises from a grand master who taught martial arts in India.

Our bodies are approximately 70 percent water content. If the body is 70 to 80 percent water content do you really need to eat a high solid food content? Do you need to clog your body, and blood vessels with solids, fats, and greasy food? No; we need to eat foods which are 70 to 80 percent water content-basically fruits, vegetables, fresh juices, and water. Most of us need to drink at least 2.5 liters of water (or its equivalent in liquid form) a day. Water intake may vary based upon the weather, exercise, fluid loss, etc.

Here is a chart on the percentage of water in some common foods.[i]

	Water content
Iceberg lettuce	96%
Radishes, celery	94%
Watermelon	93%
Cabbage (uncooked)	92%
Carrots, beets, broccoli	91%
Oranges	88%
Milk	87%
Cereals (cooked)	87%
Apples	85%
Potatoes (boiled)	80%
Bananas	76%
Corn	74%
Chicken (boiled)	71%
Fish (baked)	68%
Prunes (cooked)	66%
Beef (lean)	60%
Cheese	40%
Bread	36%
Cake (sponge)	32%
Butter	16%

Your solids should include a moderate amount of protein and carbohydrates, and the fats should be used sparingly. Follow the formula of the food pyramid and remember to include 70 to 80 percent water-content foods in your diet. When you write down your goal of losing weight and maintaining an appropriate weight, write down the course of action that you will have to take. One action is to pick up appropriate food at grocery stores rather than stopping for fast food and getting hamburgers. **Remember diseases caused by clogging blood vessels are still the number one cause of death in**

IMPROVING ENERGY AND HEALTH

United States. Learn to not clog your body. You would not do that to the fuel injector of your car.

Food guide pyramid

(Source: USDA's Food Guide Pyramid booklet prepared by Human Nutrition Information services MD 20782)[ii]

Do this simple exercise. For the next seven days write down everything you eat and drink. Write down what percentage of the food eaten was natural food compared to what was processed food. Write down what percentage of the food eaten had a high solid content compared to the food with high water content. Americans eat a lot more processed food, a lot more salt, and a lot more sugar than the body needs. 60 percent of Americans are overweight. Make a list of actions you take each day to keep your body in excellent shape.

In my seminars I ask, " Do you drive an automobile?" Most people say "yes," and then I ask, "What is the capacity of your automobile to haul a load?" They reply about a half-ton. I continue, "Would you put a one-ton load in a vehicle that is supposed to haul only a half-ton?" The audience replies "no." I query, "Why not?" They answer something on the order of, "The truck will wear out quicker if you have a heavier load." I ask, "Then why would you overload your own body?" The audience always replies that they never thought of that before, and that it makes sense-if we overload our bodies, they will wear out quicker."

In millions of people, diseases like joint pains and high blood pressure are caused by an unhealthy lifestyle. Fatigue, tiredness, and lack of energy, are all caused by a combination of lifestyle factors and perceived stress.

Let us examine what will happen to our bodies if we are overweight by thirty to forty pounds or more. Our bodies must carry the extra pounds which will be an added burden to all our weight-bearing joints, specifically ankle joints, knee joints, hips, and back. Our joints will wear out quicker due to carrying this excess weight, causing pain in many joints. What do most people do when they have pain in their joints? They end up going to a physician, paying money to be examined, and maybe having x-rays taken. In most cases they end up on a pain medication from the non-steroidal anti-inflammatory group. As long as you are overweight and continue to have joint pains you will end up taking these medications indefinitely.

When you take non-steroidal anti-inflammatory medications for years they can cause stomach upset and in some cases ulcer disease. What would you do next? You will go back to the doctor again complaining of stomach pain. The doctor certainly will examine you to earn his fee. You will then be advised to come back for a specific test-possibly a gastroscopy-for several hundred dollars more. You will be given sedation for this procedure and shown some nice pictures of the inside of your stomach and gastrointestinal tract. By this time you feel you have found a solution to your problem, which are more pills like ranitidine or cimetidine.

Who is losing thousands of dollars and ending up on pills? When you take ranitidine or cimetidine for many years, some may have side effects. This is just the beginning of a long chain of events, which will cost you thousands of dollars. When you carry extra weight your muscles have to carry unnecessary weight, causing fatigue and tiredness. Your heart and lungs have to work harder to supply energy to the excess tissue in the body. Your heart and lungs are going to wear out more quickly. When you are tired and fatigued you may not have energy to spend time with your children and loved ones. If your spouse sees you always fatigued it may put a strain on your relationship. This, with other destructive habits **(like TGIF syndrome)** may cause conflict in your relationship. Many people may go for counseling, costing hundreds of dollars, to find out why there is marital conflict. Who is losing again? One of my patients said, "Doc, I do not pay the doctor's bill, my insurance company pays it." I asked him a question "Who pays the health insurance companies?" He replied, "I guess all of us." And if you are using Medicaid, Medicare or a county health care system, we all as taxpayers pay for it.

Over time your arteries are clogged with grease and excess salt, which in turn may lead to high blood pressure. Unmanaged high blood pressure may cause a stroke or heart attack. When you are having a stroke or heart attack, what happens to your spouse? She gets anxious and frightened and calls 9-1-1. You go on a joy ride for just six hundred dollars or more in an ambulance with sirens roaring and IVs stuck in your arms and you are hooked up to a monitor with paramedics calling the hospital Emergency Room. **The fun has just begun.**

You are brought to a modern Emergency Room, in a frightened state. Many nurses and doctors hook you up to more monitors, collect blood, and then start IV fluids. They tell you they have to do a bunch more tests to figure out what is going on with you. The ER bill has just cost you thousands of dollars in just a few hours. Then you will be told they are not sure what is going on with you so they have to admit you for observation to the intensive care unit just for many more thousand dollars.

You will be greeted in the intensive care unit by more medical students, more resident doctors, more specialists, more nurses, and other therapists. You will have more tests for a few thousand dollars more. After a couple of days you will be told that you have had a mild heart attack. Then you will be discharged home with medications. You come home worried that you might have another heart attack, questioning yourself whether you can be active, keep your job, have sex, etc. You worry about the side effects caused by the new medications. By this time you have lost thousands of dollars and are on several medications. Your loved ones and you worry about your health. This all could have been prevented in most cases by the simple measures of eating healthily and doing regular exercise. *An ounce of prevention is better than wasting thousands of dollars and taking pounds of pills.*

Deaths due to cardiovascular disorders rank #1 for middle-aged persons in the United States.[iii] **Consider how many people are clogging their arteries with guess what? Greasy foods. Most fast foods are deep fried and high in fat and/or salt content.**

Let us go back to the lessons we learned in Chapter 1. Do not reinvent the wheel. There are people on this earth who live a long, healthy life, up to 110 or 120 years. They are not on a bunch of pills. They are still active physically and mentally. They are not labeled senile. There are people in the mountains of Abhkasia in Russia, people in the United States, and people in other parts of the world sharing common lifestyles which make them live longer, healthier lives without being on medication. If you and I can find out their recipe for living longer, looking younger, and maintaining an active life, and we follow the recipe these people use, we can create the same results. **Following are the ingredients of their recipes:**

IMPROVING ENERGY AND HEALTH

1. They do not have the same concept of time as people with TGIF syndrome. They do not live with the concepts of weekends and TGIF.
2. They eat naturally-grown food. (Some of them may grow their own food.) Their carbohydrates include pasta, rice, or freshly baked homemade bread. Their food is:
   —Naturally 70 to 80 percent water content with plenty of fruits, fresh vegetables, and juices.
   —High in protein.
   —Low in fat content
3. They maintain their body weight throughout their lives without much weight fluctuation.
4. Their alcohol consumption is minimal.
5. They drink only a small amount of caffeine.
6. They do not perceive aging as getting old and senile.
   —They take pride in getting older, which they call getting wiser and becoming more mature. Their family members cherish them. As grandparents they spend time with their grandkids.
   —There is a major difference between the belief systems of the people in the mountains of Abhkasia and the people in the USA. How are you treated in America when you get older? As if you are senile and useless to society.
7. They sleep seven to eight hours at a natural sleeping time, which is during the night, and are early risers.
8. They are free from anxiety, worry, and depression.
9. They are independent and like to manage their own affairs.
10. They remain physically active in later life and continue to work as they get older.
11. They like to make their own decisions and do not like to be bound by the restraints of organization.
12. They maintain physical activity by daily walking, or working on a farm, or by regular exercise, and remain in good physical shape performing the activities of daily life.
13. They are not engrossed with thoughts of dying.

14. They can enjoy simple things in life and they are optimists.
15. They are flexible about changes in life and do not complain about change.
    —Remember palm trees survive high winds of hurricane by being flexible compared to an oak tree collapsing by being rigid.
16. They keep themselves intellectually active. They take an interest in current events.

One weekend I visited a farmer in northwestern Missouri who is 71 years old and still actively working every day on his farm. He said "Hemant, we don't realize that it's the weekend until you come from the city and tell us it is the weekend. We wake up early in the morning and go to work whether it is Monday or Sunday." This farmer woke up each day just before sunrise and went to bed at ten o'clock. It did not make any difference to him if it was cloudy or sunny, he continued his work. He certainly does not embrace the TGIF syndrome.

Why not follow this recipe from people who live longer and more healthily? As we learned in Chapter 1, **do not reinvent the wheel-find a recipe.** Find a recipe and follow the recipe exactly and you will have the same results. If we follow the recipe of people who are living longer and more healthily, who look younger and have an active physical and mental life, we will have the same results, without taking too many pills. If we follow the recipe these people have mastered for living longer and healthier we can create an abundance of both physical and mental energy.

I ask my audiences, "If you have a cat or a dog at home, would you let your dog or cat smoke, drink beer, eat a sack of potato chips and watch TV for eight hours a day?" Most audiences look serious and reply that they would never do such a thing to their cats and dogs. Then I ask them, "If you wouldn't allow your cats and dogs to smoke, to drink booze, to eat greasy food, and lay around lazily watching TV then why would you do such a thing to your own body?" Most audiences reply that they never thought about it this way. When it comes to the treatment of our pets, we would give them correct food, take them for a walk or exercise, give them adequate rest and not allow them to use drugs, drink booze, or smoke cigarettes. I have observed that *people take better care of their cats and dogs than themselves.*

Let us treat ourselves well, and create an abundance of energy by following a simple recipe. Let us create energy, which will be beneficial to us, our family, fellow human beings, and the planet Earth.

Lessons learned in this chapter:

1. **The essential source of energy is oxygen. We can access it by deep diaphragmatic breathing.**
2. **Deep breathing helps to provide increased oxygen to every cell in your body.**
3. **Deep breathing with long exhalation will help to cleanse the toxic waste products from the body.**
4. **Regular exercise and deep breathing helps improve circulation, resulting in a plentiful supply of oxygen to each cell in the body.**
5. **Your body is 70 to 80 percent water content. Do not clog it with solids or fatty foods. Eating 70 to 80 percent water-content foods will help to keep your system unclogged. Water is the best solvent on Earth and helps to eliminate toxic wastes from the body.**
6. **Processed foods may have pollutants in them. Eat fresh, unprocessed foods.**
7. **Adequate rest is essential for an energetic life. Life in nature is a combination of rest and activity. Get adequate physical and mental rest combined with adequate physical and mental activity.**
8. **Follow the recipe of people who live longer, active, healthier lives.**

HEMANT THAKUR, MD

*The key to creating plenty of energy and improved health
is to make simple lifestyle changes.*

---

i U.S. Department of Agriculture
ii U.S. Department of Agriculture. Food Guide Pyramid Booklet. Hyattsville, Maryland:
   Human Nutrition Information Service. Web site address:
   http://www.pueblo.gsa.gov/cic_text/food/food-pyramid/main.htm
iii Current Medical Diagnosis and Treatment. 33rd annual rev. Edited by Lawrence M. Tierney, Jr.,
   M.D., Stephen J. McPhee, M.D., Maxine A. Papadakis, M.D., et al. Norwalk, Conn.:
   Appleton & Lange, 1994.
Improving Energy and Health

Chapter 18

Meditation

Meditation is not magic or mysticism. It is useful for people from all walks of life. You do not have to be a monk or go to an Ashram to practice meditation. I have been a physician, an officer in the United States Army Reserve, a businessman, teacher, and parent and have performed various roles in life. Meditation has improved my performance in many areas of life. The physical and emotional effects of mediation are benefits, separate from any spiritual benefit.

Most of you have been to a lake. If you observe the water in the lake when it is still and calm it is clear. When the water is turbulent, it is not clear. Our minds are constantly thinking about something. The mind constantly entertains a turbulence of thoughts. If we learn to hold our minds still, then the mind will become clear. Many people think meditation is just for relaxation or for those on a spiritual quest. Meditation has numerous psychological and physical benefits. These benefits will help us in many other areas of life including work, relationships and improving concentration on any task. It teaches us how to focus our minds.

There are several techniques and stages of meditation. The techniques I practice involve sitting in a quiet place with my back straight in a comfortable position. I usually prefer some natural sounds around me. I then concentrate on breathing, taking deep breaths in and out. Focusing on breathing helps to clear the mind. Now you begin........... Your mind may wander from time to time to different thoughts. These thoughts can be memories, worries, thoughts about your relationships, your plans, your fantasies, etc. Just bring your mind back to the breath. You have a fundamental contract with yourself to focus on breathing, and everything else is irrelevant at this time.i Whenever you start floating into some other thoughts, you must refocus your attention on breathing. This technique is known as mindfulness. Initially when you first begin to meditate, your mind may wander off frequently and you may have difficulty holding your mind still. Your mind may want to think about the worries of the day, your bills, your relationships, past events, fantasies, finances, the future, etc. As you practice more and more, you will start becoming aware of variations in your breathing patterns and rhythms that you had never perceived in the past. The utmost attention to breathing will help clear your mind. Some other techniques use a mantra, which can be any word in any language with a positive meaning, and in that case, one focuses on the mantra. Your mantra does not have to be a Sanskrit word.ii

Most meditation methods are similar in some respects and usually involve focusing the mind on breathing or a mantra and clearing the mind of any thoughts. Meditation techniques teach transforming consciousness. Right attitude and right aspiration is more important than the technique of meditation. Leave your mind in a natural space instead of the turbulence of thoughts. One can find more information on various meditation techniques by going to the public library. The single invariable component for altering consciousness through any meditation technique is retraining the attention either by mindfulness or through concentration. Meditation can be part of your daily activity and one does not have to be on any spiritual path to practice meditation. Meditation has been used in one form or another universally in all different religious backgrounds. Even though meditation is used widely for relaxation, meditation and relaxation are not one and the same. Meditation teaches us to refocus our attention. Thus it helps us to improve cognitive ability related to improved focus and concentration.

MEDITATION

Meditation has profound effects on immune functioning. Regular meditation has been shown to decrease the number of colds, decrease blood pressure, and improve sleep.

People try to relax by going on vacation, to a movie, watching TV, drinking at a bar, or going shopping. Even when one goes on vacation the mind is trying to rush to get on plane, find a spot on the beach, or worry about sunburn. When you watch a movie or TV your mind wonders about all the events taking place in the movie. If you go to a bar, you think about whom you are going to meet and what interactions will take place. If you go shopping, you have to go through the hustle and bustle of crowds in the shopping center, find a parking place, stand in lines and think about an infinite number of things. Learn to take a break for yourself. Life is full of rest and activity. If we learn to rest our minds, we can use them better during the times of activities. Nature teaches us that all the time. Nature has night and day, winter and summer. When we are constantly struggling with meeting deadlines and pushing against our inherent nature, it can cause stress. Stress can induce anxiety, depression, restless sleep, nervousness, fear, increased blood pressure, gastrointestinal and other physical symptoms. Learn to pause and calm your mind. This can be done without any pills through meditation, at least for a period of time.

Many research studies show that meditation helps to decrease blood pressure. Mild hypertension, especially, can be brought to normal by a combination of meditation and the techniques we described in Chapter17. At an American Heart Association meeting, Dr. Dean Ornish of Sausalito, California presented dramatic evidence of the effects of concentrated relaxation on the reversal of heart disease in people with hypertension and clogged arteries.iii Their program included a regimen of Yoga, meditation, low-fat vegetarian diets, and exercise. It sure beats paying a physician hundreds of dollars and taking bunches of pills. A personal friend of mine was on antihypertensive medications for more than ten years (and also taking other medications for side effects from his first medication). He managed to get off all the medications after practicing these techniques for six months and following other lifestyle changes suggested in Chapter 17. To his surprise his blood pressure has been running 110/70, which is very good after having had a history of hypertension for more than ten years.

My baseline pulse runs about 54 since I started practicing meditation and following these lifestyle changes, despite a very active life. Studies done at Harvard and the University of Massachusetts reported regular meditation caused a reduction in blood pressure for hundreds of patients with a history of hypertension. The National Institute of Health recommended in their report in the early 1980s, that meditation with salt restriction, low-fat diets, and daily exercise helped to reduce blood pressure in patients with hypertension. If you like taking pills and making the health care industry rich, then it is your choice. I personally would not like to be on bunch of pills for the rest of my life if I can avoid it by simple lifestyle changes.

Mediation has been shown to decrease anxiety, and improve sleep. Studies done at Harvard by Gary Schwartz showed much lower levels of anxiety among meditators compared to nonmeditators.iv Meditators can deal with life stresses better than nonmeditators. In my personal life I have been able to increase my energy for the activities of the various roles I have, despite the problems of running a business, coping with the changing health care industry, and assuming the responsibilities of being a parent. Meditation does not sedate people; it actually makes them livelier. I have more energy and humor while doing the seminars since I have made changes in my lifestyle and started meditating.

Meditation trains us to improve our focus and attention. You may realize that for most people their minds wander from thought to thought. The human brain is faced with thousands of stimuli at any

MEDITATION

given instant. Meditation helps us to sharpen our attention and focus. Concentrated focus is very powerful when it comes down to achieving a goal. Ask a martial artist how he breaks a wooden board-it has more to do with concentrated focus than just pure strength. The sharpening of attention continues beyond the actual meditation in daily activities. The calmness caused by meditation continues beyond the time of meditation.

Meditation has many benefits. It helps you to focus your mind well. It helps to lower blood pressure. It helps to improve your health and health habits.[v] It helps to slow down the aging process. It helps to increase self-actualization. It decreases the incidence of disease.[vi] It increases creativity. It increases energy and vitality. It reduces negative personality characteristics. It helps to create better health habits. It helps to improve health and muscular systems. Transcendental meditation can improve the health of the cardiovascular, respiratory, nervous, endocrine, and immune systems and reverse the aging process.[vii]

There have been over five hundred scientific studies conducted at more than two hundred universities and research institutions in thirty countries.[viii] They have proven the effectiveness of meditation and associated health programs. For reference, refer to scientific papers reprinted in the scientific research of Maharishi's Transcendental Meditation and TM Sidhi program collective papers, volumes 1 through 6. There has been research done at Harvard Medical School, Princeton University, Stanford Medical School, the University of Chicago, the University of Michigan Medical School, the University of California at Berkeley, the University of New South Wales, Australia, and many other places. The list of research articles and scientific papers showing the detailed benefits of meditation is vast and beyond the scope of this book.

Meditation has numerous benefits without taking any medication. There is clear validation that people who practice meditation on an ongoing basis exhibit better health. They have shown a decrease in health problems, a decrease in hospital visits, and fewer doctor visits. Learn to give your mind a break and create calmness within yourself. The ability to create calmness is within yourself. Life is a combination of rest and activity. **Meditation will give you the ability to tap within yourself to earn numerous benefits and create calmness within you**.

> *The art of resting the mind, and the power of dismissing from it all care and worry is probably one of the secrets of energy in our great men.*
> *(Captain J. A. Hadfield)*

---

i Sogyal Rinpoche. Ancient Wisdom for a Modern World. (Audio Book) Carson, Calif.: Hay House, 1995.

ii Paul Wilson. The Calm Technique, Meditation without Magic or Mysticism. Australia: Penguin Books, 1995.

iii Daniel Goleman, Ph.D. Art of Meditation. Los Angeles: Audio Renaissance Tapes. New York: Distr. By St. Martin's Press Inc., 1989.

iv See note iii above.

v Scientific Research on the Maharishi Transcendental Meditation and TM-Sidhi Programs. Maharishi University of Management: Fairfield, Iowa

vi See note v above.

vii See note v above.

viii See note v above.

Chapter 19

Power Within Self

The ability to create anything we want is within us!

So far, you have been given a lot of different tools and techniques for achieving phenomenal results in your life. Most of these techniques are designed to empower you and help you achieve your full potential. Basically, you can create anything you want just by applying the techniques and principles presented in the previous chapters. For example, if someone looks at you a certain way, and you start telling yourself he was giving you a dirty look, you will start to generate a lot of negative ideas about his "dirty look." You may tell yourself he doesn't like your tie, your skin color, your hair, or even your shoes. The point is that all of this happens inside your head. Nobody made it happen to you. And all of it is fantasy based on false evidence produced by you, regardless of how close to reality it is or isn't.

Even if you decided the man had not given you a dirty look at all, but in fact liked you, this new idea would still be a fantasy created by you inside your head. If I believe a woman has a crush on me-whether or not she does have a crush on me-that belief is a creation of my mind. I may think she likes my skin color, my clothes, or the way I talk. Whatever the reasons, my belief that she has a crush on me is only my perception and my reactions may not be based on reality.

The point is that all ideas originate within the mind. Good or bad, heaven or hell, all ideas are created within us. If you create the idea that you're an evil person, that idea originates within you. Regardless of the event or situation, your reactions, good or bad originate within you.

The idea to find another job, to go to college and get an education, to be social or not, is created within you. Anything you create comes from an idea that originated from somewhere inside your own head. If you know how to tap into your creative potential, you can and will achieve just about anything you want.

Each one of us has the ability to teach ourselves anything and to make ourselves believe anything. Once you trust, you will start gathering evidence to support this. If you study some of the great leaders, such as Martin Luther King, Jr. or Mahatma Gandhi, you will find they were not motivated by self-interest or a need to be seen as great leaders. Each was motivated by a need to serve and help humanity.

If you teach a kid he can only be "cool" if he wears a certain brand-name pair of shoes, and you tell him you cannot afford to buy them for him, what is he likely to do? Depending on how important it is to him to be cool, he may resort to violence to get the money for the shoes or to get another kid's shoes. Similarly, if you teach your kid that he is only great if he has a jacket with the brand-name logo on it, and you can't afford to buy it for him, he may become violent and actually kill someone for it and end up under arrest.

Who ultimately pays for the problems of our younger generation? We all do, at a cost of about $40,000 a year to keep someone in prison. And, if a juvenile ends up going to a prison for ten years, then it costs us about $400,000, excluding the legal fees that usually go hand in hand. The total cost can be as high as half a million dollars, all because a kid was conditioned to believe that he needed a certain jacket or pair of shoes to be cool.

POWER WITHIN SELF

Many of us are prisoners of this kind of disempowering conditioning. Our imprisonment keeps us from using our full potential to benefit ourselves, others and our planet as a whole. Our dependency on others' validation, approval and acceptance for a sense of self-worth is a conditioned response. We learned to seek others' approval and acceptance, and continuing to respond out of this dependency can only become an Action for Disaster. How? Because in the process of obtaining my sense of worth from other people or other things, I end up hurting others.

Think about the many millions of conditioned responses we produce daily, and about the many more we're exposed to. For example, say I'm living in a three-bedroom house, and my neighbor next door builds a house with five bedrooms. I have been conditioned to believe that I cannot feel good about myself until I have a house at least as big as my neighbor's. My self-worth is dependent on whether I have the bigger house.

In the United States, we have more material wealth than any other country in the world. Are most Americans happy? No, because we're always striving to obtain or achieve more materially. Our minds are conditioned to strive for bigger and better, which obviously doesn't guarantee happiness or self-esteem. Instead, the striving for more just keeps us imprisoned in our own conditioning.

Another example: I have all kinds of certificates hanging on a wall in my office. I have numerous titles, such as director, major, assistant clinical professor, and president of a corporation. If I allow myself to become overly attached to these titles, and believe that my value is dependent on the number and status of my titles, then I become a prisoner of my own conditioning. My notions about self-worth may have come from my parents, my church, my neighbors, or my school community. If I do not have these titles, how am I likely to feel? Probably angry, resentful, trapped, hopeless, and helpless.

I recently saw a commercial for a hair salon that communicated the basic message, "If you want to feel good, this is the only place to have your hair done." The owner was trying to manipulate specific feelings and behavioral responses from the target audience, which in turn would leave each individual a prisoner of an external condition. The message is communicated in such a way that any woman watching the commercial would believe that she had no worth unless she got her hair done at this particular salon.

We get into a rat race and have to have the biggest house, the best car, and the most beautiful hairstyle. If we do not get what we believe we cannot survive without, then we feel empty and trapped by our own conditioning. We can even have a conditioned response to our own race or religion. If we are black or a person of color, we may believe we are no good. Who created this conditioned response? We did. We did it to ourselves, and the antidote is deep inside ourselves.

You can create anything you want as long as you learn to manage yourself. Focus on your needs and goals as well as the needs and goals that will benefit humanity. Each time you make a choice or prepare to take action, ask yourself this question: How is this choice/action/decision going to benefit me, my family, my neighbor, and all humanity? If you are able to pursue actions that are beneficial to your family, your neighbors, or all of humanity, then you cannot go wrong. Everyone will benefit, and you are able to put an end to your imprisonment.

Nature does not withhold. It does not say, "Do not use this water for a while." If it did, we would all be dead. It is only man who acts this way. The resources on Earth have not changed. The same amount of carbon, nitrogen and oxygen exists today as they did millions of years ago. This same carbon, nitrogen, and oxygen make up our food, furniture, cars, and even us. We are in a constant process of exchanging these atoms. We have also become more technologically advanced. We

POWER WITHIN SELF

now make cars that can run for one hundred miles on two gallons of gas. We have computers to do the tasks that used to take one hundred people to do. We can dig a hole in minutes with heavy equipment when it used to take hours to dig the same hole by hand. We have become efficient in using the resources available on earth, but not sophisticated enough to manage them well-there is still scarcity. Man is the creator of this scarcity. Once again I say, *the problems of mankind are created by man and the solutions to them are within us.*

So far in this chapter, we have learned that the ability to create anything is within each one of us. Feelings of joy, happiness, anger, fear, or peace are created within us. Everything around us, from furniture to cars, started as a thought in someone's head.

The second thing we learned in this chapter is the way we behave, the way we react, and the way we perceive things, are conditioned responses. This idea is shown in above diagram. We are a product of numerous conditioned responses. The lines between the bigger circle and smaller circle indicate the bondage of conditioned responses. The circles in the periphery indicate how we react or perceive different events and objects based upon our past conditioning. **If we master how to break down the disempowering conditioned responses we can have ultimate freedom and power to create anything we want.**

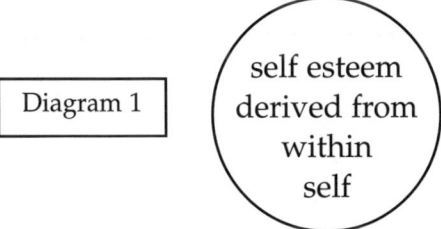

Diagram 1

HEMANT THAKUR, MD

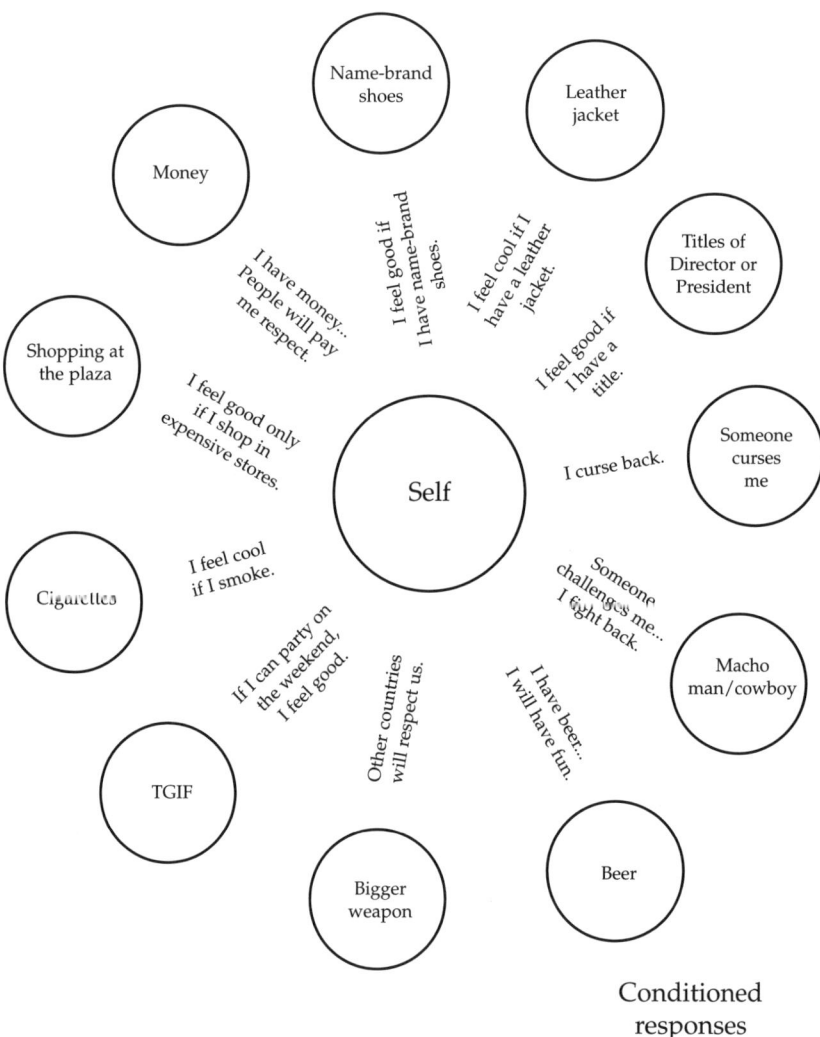

Self: The ability to create anything we want is within us!

What is the world made of?

If we analyze a human body, a piece of rock, a plant and an animal and break them down into their most basic elements, what will be left are tiny atoms of carbon, hydrogen, oxygen, nitrogen, and a few other minerals. Everything around us, including our bodies, is made up of these atoms. We are constantly exchanging these atoms with animals, plants, humans, and other objects in the environment. So what is the difference between the atoms of the pavement and the grass growing next to it? When the spring arrives, the grass starts growing. When it is winter, the grass stops growing and becomes dormant. So the grass is aware of the changes in weather and light. A rock is not capable of the same level of awareness that the grass or the plant kingdom has.

Take the example of any animal or bird and compare it to grass or members of the plant kingdom. If we cut grass or we cut some fruit from trees, the tree does not start attacking or biting us. The tree does not scream at us. But try doing this to a bird or any animal or try to take away their offspring and you will realize that they will try to protect their offspring even to the point of attacking you. Birds also build nests or find protected shelters for their offspring. Thus the birds and animals have a better awareness than the plant kingdom. At the next level are human beings. We have awareness not only of the changes in the weather, and of protecting our offspring, we are also able to accomplish millions of different tasks from manufacturing cars and satellites, to creating artificial foods and figuring out how to grow better crops. We create wars and we are aware of millions of different things. Many species do not have the same level of awareness. Thus, as human beings we have awareness and information in many more areas than other species on Earth.

Radioisotope studies have found that the human body is constantly replacing atoms all the time. We are exchanging atoms in the form of air, water, and food, which comes from the Earth. These radioisotope studies have shown that our skin is replaced once a month and the skeleton is replaced every three months. Even the atoms in the brain cells are replaced every few weeks, the liver cells are replaced every six weeks, and the stomach lining is replaced every five days.i The molecules of DNA atoms get replaced every few weeks. If every cell in the body is replaced in less than two years by new atoms how does one continue to manufacture the same white or brown skin, or red or black hair? We are putting similar atoms in our bodies when we eat food. We drink the same water and we inhale the same oxygen from the same atmosphere. We live in the same community. My friend Bernie produces red hair and I produce black hair. Despite the replacement of cells in my body in less than two years, I continue to think the way I was taught. I continue to speak with an Asian accent. My friend Bernie continues to speak with an Australian accent. I also continue to reproduce the scar on my skin from a previous injury, which happened twenty years ago on that spot.

A patient of mine asked me during a seminar, "Doc, if you are saying that our body replaces every atom in less than two years, how come I still have arthritis in my neck and knee joints?" It should disappear since the atoms have been exchanged. Believe it or not, there is an answer to this puzzle. Even though every atom in our body is replaced we continue to carry the same information and awareness in the replacement cell. For example, my daughter Pooja is allergic to nuts. She develops asthma and other severe allergic symptoms when she is exposed to certain nuts and pollen. She asked me, "Dad, if you are telling me that every cell in my body is replaced in less than two years, how come I continue to be allergic to these nuts, and how come I do not get rid of these allergies?" Somehow every cell in the body continues the same awareness and information to reproduce this allergic reaction when she is exposed to nuts and other substances to which she is allergic.

POWER WITHIN SELF

So where is this memory and awareness and information? Is it at the material level? I ask these questions of my audiences, "If you weigh me while I am talking and alive how much would I weigh on a precise scale if I weigh 144 pounds and 6 ounces?" The answer is obvious. Then I ask the next question, "If I die a moment later and you weigh me again, how much would I weigh?" The audience says, "You would weigh the same." So what made me walk and talk and communicate and take actions, and coordinate six trillion reactions in one second? I didn't change physically between life and death. So what made me coordinate and process all of these actions? Is it a material thing? What enables me or any of us to do all these things-seeing, talking, walking, communicating with others, performing thousands of actions-is within all of us, and **it is non-material**.

Most of you have worked with computers and fax machines, and have seen scientists manage satellite movements of vehicles on Mars. Say I am sitting in front of a videophone in Kansas City and my friend Bernie is sitting in front of a videophone in Australia. My image and voice is picked up by the videophone and transmitted to Australia through phone lines. The computer camera creates my image and gathers my voice and reproduces it on the other side of this planet in a matter of seconds. Is there any physical connection or material flowing between me in Kansas City and Bernie in Australia? No, there is no physical material flowing between the two computer videophones. There is invisible energy and it transmits this information from one side of the planet to the other side in few seconds, and reproduces our images as well as our voices.

Scientists have been able to break down atoms into minute particles and observe them in a particle accelerator. What they found was that even the atoms of iron or any material which looks solid, when it is broken down into these tiny particles called quarks, leptons, photons, etc.,ii look like a huge void, such as you see on a starry night. A big darkness with millions of particles like stars moving in a precise manner. What makes a difference between an atom of iron and an atom of silver is the energy and information between these particles and the way they are moving in this huge void. So what makes the difference between atoms of iron and silver is the difference between the energy and the information they carry. Each atom of iron or silver is more than 99 percent hollow or non-material.iii Quarks and electrons are smaller than 10 to the power of (-18) meters; it is possible they have no size at all. It is possible that quarks and electrons are not fundamental but are composites of more fundamental particles. The following diagram illustrates the scale of these things and the breaking down of atoms to the smallest particles known. (Courtesy of Lawrence Berkeley National Laboratories, Berkeley, California.

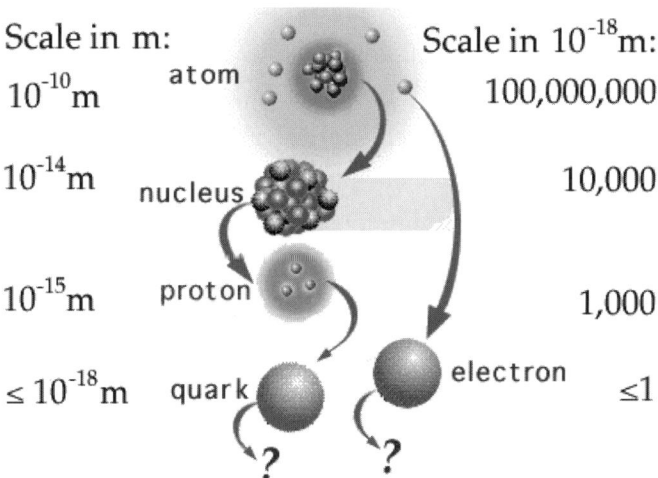

If you compare the smallest object in the universe, the atom, with the largest object, a galaxy, they are both more than 99 percent hollow. See their fascinating images on the back cover of the book.

Returning to the subject of the self, we came to the conclusion that at the material or physical level there is not much difference between death and life, there is not much difference between George and Sally, there is not much difference between Bill Clinton and Sadaam Hussein. What makes each unique is the information and energy within them and the conditioned pattern of this information and energy. Thus the ability to create anything is within us and we all possess that. If we master managing the information and the energy within us we can create whatever we want. The ability to create heaven or hell, the ability to create demons or angels, peace and happiness, or anger and hatred, is within us. We all possess it and it is within ourselves.

Think of the power that is in the universe, moving the earth, growing trees. And it is the same power within you.
(Charles Chaplin)

"*The problems of mankind are created by man. The solutions to those problems are within us.*"
Hemant Thakur, M.D.

Mind Body Soul in Service to Humanity.

---

i Deepak Chopra. Ageless Body, Timeless Mind. Harmony Books, 1993.
ii The Particle Adventure. Lawrence Berkeley National Laboratories. Berkeley, CA. http://ccwww.kek.jp/pdg/cpep/atom_scale.html
iii See note ii above.

Goals	Deadlines
1.	
2.	
3.	
4.	
5.	
6.	
7.	
8.	
9.	
10.	

MEGA MIND

Goals   **Deadlines**

1._____

2._____

3._____

4._____

5._____

6._____

7._____

8._____

9._____

10._____

Bibliography

The following is a selected bibliography that offers insights into some of the topics represented in Mega-Mind, Path to Success and Freedom.

Ader, Robert, David L. Felten, Nicholas Cohen. Psychoneuroimmunology. 2nd ed. New York: Academic Press, 1991.

American Heart Association. Leading Causes of Death in the United States: 1994 Estimates. Information provided by Greater Kansas City Division, P.O. Box 917, Shawnee Mission, Kansas 66201-0917.

Bhaktivedanta, A. C. Swami Prabhupada. Bhagavad-Gita As It Is. 6th Printing. Los Angeles: Bhaktivedanta Book Trust, 1994.

Bits & Pieces, The Magazine that Motivates the World. Volume R/No. 29. Fairfield, NJ: The Economic Press, Inc., 1997.

Chopra, Deepak. Ageless Body, Timeless Mind. Harmony Books, 1993.

Chopra, Deepak. Seven Spiritual Laws of Success. San Rafael, California: Amber Allen Publishing, New World Library, 1993.

Current Medical Diagnosis and Treatment. 33rd annual rev. Edited by Lawrence M. Tierney, Jr., M.D., Stephen J. McPhee, M.D., Maxine A. Papadakis, M.D., et al. Norwalk, Conn.: Appleton & Lange, 1994.

Dantzer, Robert. Stress and Immunity: What Have We Learned from Psychoneuroimmunology? Bordeaux, France: Neurobiologic

Integrative, INSERM U394, Pages 43-46.

Dilts, Robert, John Grinder, Richard Bandler, Leslie Bandler and Judith DeLozier. Neuro-Linguistic Programming: The Study of the Structure of Excellence. Cupertino, CA: Meta Publications, 1980.

Frankl, Victor E. Man's Search For Meaning: an Introduction to Logotherapy. 4th edition. Boston: Simon & Schuster, Beacon Press, 1984.

Gilman, Alfred Goodman, Louis S. Goodman, Alfred Gilman. Goodman and Gilman's, The Pharmacological Basis of Therapeutics. 6th ed. New York: Macmillan Publishing Co. Inc., 1980.

Goleman, Daniel, Ph.D. Art of Meditation. Los Angeles: Audio Renaissance Tapes. New York: Distr. St. Martin's Press Inc., 1989.

Hafen, Brent Q., Keith J. Karren, Kathryn Frandsen and N. Lee Smith. Mind Body Health: The Effects of Attitude, Emotions and Relationships. Boston: Allyn & Bacon, a Simon & Schuster Company. 1996.

Halverson, Glen A., M.D. Stop Burning a Hole in Your Brain, Revolutionary Nutrient Restores and Protects Your Health. (Audiotape) and O.P.C. 300 Plus (Information on Resveratrol). Lumenhealth Enterprises, P.O. Box 1677, Topanga, CA 90290, 1997.

Hyman, Ronald T. Strategic Questioning. Englewood Cliffs, NJ: Prentice Hall, 1979.

Illinois Transportation Department, National Highway and Traffic Safety Board. Obtained statistics on number of drinks and blood alcohol level.

Kaplan, Harold, M.D. and Benjamin Saddock, M.D. Synopsis of Psychiatry, Behavioral Sciences Clinical Psychiatry. Senior editor: Robert Cancro M.D., Med. D. Sc. 6th ed. Baltimore, Maryland: Williams & Wilkins, 1988.

Lawrence Berkeley National Laboratories. The Particle Adventure. Berkeley, CA. Web site address:
http://ccwww.kek.jp/pdg/cpep/atom_scale.html

MADD (Mothers Against Drunk Driving). Don't Call Me Lucky. Also other information provided by the Heartland Chapter, Shawnee Mission, Kansas 66208.

Maharishi Mahesh Yogi. Maharishi Forum of Natural Law and National Law for Doctors. 2nd ed. Canada: Age of Enlightenment Publications, Maharishi Vedic University, 1996.

Martin, Paul R., M.D. The Healing Mind, the Vital Links between Brain and Behavior, Immunity and Disease. New York: St. Martin's Press, 1998.

Missouri Department of Mental Health, Division of Alcohol and Drug Abuse. Jefferson City, Missouri.

Faulkner, Charles, Gerry Schmidt, Robert McDonald, Tim Hallbom, Suzi Smith, Kelly Gerling, Ph.D. NLP The New Technology of Achievement. Audiotapes. Chicago: Nightingale Conant

Oxford English Dictionary, Compact Edition. 25th ed. Oxford: Oxford University Press, 1986.

Powell, Colin with Joseph E. Persico. My American Journey. New York: Random House, 1995.

Rinpoche, Sogyal. Ancient Wisdom for a Modern World. (Audio Book) Carson, California: Hay House, 1995.

Robbins, Anthony. Unlimited Power. Ballantine Books, Div. Of Random House, 1986.

Scientific Research on the Maharishi Transcendental Meditation and TM-Sidhi Programs. Maharishi University of Management: Fairfield, Iowa

Tierney, Lawrence M., Jr., Stephen J. McPhee & Maxine A. Papadakis. Current Medical Diagnosis & Treatment. 33rd ed. Norwalk, Connecticut: Appleton & Lange, 1994.

U.S. Department of Agriculture. Food Guide Pyramid Booklet. Hyattsville, Maryland: Human Nutrition Information Service. Web site address:
http://www.pueblo.gsa.gov/cic_text/food/food-pyramid/main.htm

U.S. Department of Agriculture. Home Garden Bulletin. No. 72. Hyattsville, Maryland: Human Nutrition Information Service.

U.S. Department of Health and Human Services. Alcohol and Health. National Institute on Alcohol Abuse and Alcoholism. Seventh Special Report to the U.S. Congress. Chair of editorial review board Enoch Gordis M.D. Alexandria, Virginia: Editorial Experts Inc., 1990.

Wilson, Paul. The Calm Technique, Meditation without Magic or Mysticism. Australia: Penguin Books, 1995.

The Story Behind Veterans for Humanity, Inc.

As a physician/psychiartrist, Dr. Thakur faced many tragedies with the people around him. As an example, he had a forty-five-year-old patient who was shot by a fourteen-year-old in a carjacking. The patient went into a coma and was hospitalized for more than four months, with bullet wounds in his lungs and thighs. When he was discharged, the hospital billed the state for more than $300,000 as the patient could not pay it. Dr. Thakur started wondering why a teenager would shoot a man for a $500 car, and he wondered what he could do to change this kind of behavior in people.

In another incident, twenty-five-year-old resident physician Shawn Storm was shot dead near his medical school by a sixteen-year-old teenager, leaving a grieving young widow and community of friends. Dr. Thakur was his teacher prior to this incidence. Dr. Thakur continued to ask searching questions about why a sixteen-year-old kid would shoot a man outside his house. What influence could Dr. Thakur extend to change these things?

Dr. Thakur's conclusion was to begin teaching non-violence to children and adults in the community, so they would have the tools to live very successful lives without hurting others. He formed Veterans for Humanity, Inc., a non-profit corporation, with this goal in mind.

The mission of Veterans for Humanity is to empower veterans and others by teaching them how to succeed in many areas of life. In turn, veterans and others who are trained in the classes, master these skills and become mentors throughout the community, teaching these techniques to all who are willing to learn. Veterans, through this training, develop into valued members of their communities, demonstrating success by enhancing their lives through meaningful work and supportive relationships. They involve themselves as volunteers in community activities such as neighborhood clean up, working with the elderly, Head Start programs, and many other areas. They serve as mentors for troubled youth and they participate in speakers' bureaus. The book *Mega-Mind, Path to Success and Freedom* is part of this project to help people make a success of their lives.

If you would like to contact Veterans for Humanity, please visit us at Web site: **http://www.netcam.com.au/~bernadet/MegaMind/index-4.html**